BIRTHDAY
CAKES

by
Mary Ford

WITH STEP-BY-STEP INSTRUCTIONS

Printed and bound in Great Britain by Purnell Book Productions Ltd.

ISBN 0 946429 05 7

All cake designs in this book have been previously published in either Mary Ford's 101 Cake Designs or Mary Ford's Cake Designs - Another 101

The Authors.

Mary was born in Wick Village, near Bristol. Her interest in cake icing started when her father, a flour miller, encouraged her to take up the craft.

On leaving school, therefore, Mary went straight into a bakery on a four-year apprenticeship, with a day release each week to attend a course at Bristol Technical College, where she gained her Final City and Guilds in Bread Making and Flour Confectionery.

Having moved to London to gain greater experience, Mary finally settled in Bournemouth where she started teaching cake icing in Bournemouth and Southampton Colleges. That eventually led to private tuition.

She met and married Michael and as their business increased, so ever larger premises were found to accommodate larger classes. Mary, throughout this period, continued icing cakes to order and instructing students who were arriving from all parts of the World.

Mary makes no secret of the fact that cake decoration is the consuming passion of her life. She has won innumerable awards in the craft.

Michael was born in Croydon, Surrey. His ambition to succeed in the culinary arts began at school, where he was the only boy to study cookery. This led to a three-year course in bread making and flour confectionery at Plymouth Technical College. There Michael achieved the Final City and Guilds in the subject.

He then travelled the country to further his practical experience in various hotels, restaurants and bakeries. He visited Bournemouth to work in a bakery and there met and married Mary in 1970.

His ambition to manage his own business came to fruition 12 months later when, with Mary, he created the forerunner to the Mary Ford Cake Artistry Centre.

Michael introduced a number of ideas in order to expand the company, including mail order, correspondence courses throughout the World and the development and manufacture of cake artistry tools.

A natural follow-up to the correspondence courses was the production of books on cake icing artistry for which Michael has been responsible for all the photography.

Preface

Over many years our friends and customers asked us to produce a cake icing book and this we did in 1982. That book 101 Cake Designs - proved to be a best seller and created the demand for a second book. The challenge became irresistible to us and the result was Mary Ford's Cake Designs - Another 101.

By demand, we are now producing this series of titles devoted to specialist types of cakes, selected from our first two books.

We sincerely trust this book, as well as its companion books, will give much pleasure and help to all who use them in the pursuit of excellence in cake icing artistry.

Our thanks go to Stan and Betty Oddy and all who have helped in the preparation of this book.

Michael and Mary

Introduction

The Mary Ford Story is a fairy tale come true. No waving of a magic wand has however brought about the success and quality of product which is associated with the Mary Ford Cake Artistry Centre. Hard work, dedication, perseverance and consistently high standards of product have achieved this.

Michael and Mary Ford manage their enterprise from premises in Southbourne, Bournemouth, England. From this base they bake and sell their own bread and confectionary; ice celebratory cakes to order and give, amongst other things, instruction in cake icing as well as bread, pastry, cake and chocolate making. Demonstrations in the art of cake icing are featured and the Cake Artistry Centre sells, by mail order and over the counter, all manner of cake icing equipment, decorations and raw materials.

All this is a long way from the one small room in an hotel annexe where, in 1971, Mary commenced instructing just six pupils each session. Michael and Mary progressed to their first retail outlet and then moved to their present address. To raise part of the capital they then needed, their home had to be sold - such was the faith in their own ability and urge to succeed.

The quality of the Mary Ford Centre work is a byword to professionals and amateurs alike and this book is the latest in a comprehensive list of outstanding goods to come from Mary Ford and, as is only to be expected, is produced in a highly professional and, thus, easy to follow manner.

For years now the British have led the world in cake icing artistry - especially in the use of royal icing - and our pre-eminence in this field is due solely to the skills of craftspeople like England's Mary Ford. She is an undoubted world leader in her chosen profession and, through her books on step-by-step icing instructions, has received a well earned international recognition and reputation.

To answer a growing demand for cake icing books on different subjects Mary has specially selected twenty-seven birthday cake designs from her two best selling books:

Mary Ford 101 Cake Designs

Mary Ford's Cake Designs - Another 101

Without fear of contradiction, it can be said that this beautifully produced book - containing almost 1000 coloured photographs - is a work of art in its own right. For, each of the twenty-seven cake designs featured in the book, enjoys a full-page colour photograph and every stage of each design is pictured in thirty-two step-by-step coloured photographs and supported by by easy to follow written instructions.

Other books in the series:

Novelty Cakes
Decorated Cakes
Wedding Cakes

These are outstanding books which both professional and amateur will value owning.

S & B

Contents

Reference table to cake designs.

NAME	STYLE	PAGES	FRUIT CAKE SIZES (inches)	BOARD SIZES (inches	MARZIPAN (lbs)	ROYAL ICING (lbs)	SUGAR PASTE (lbs)
ADRIAN	Square (21)	42-44	8	11	2	3	-
ALBERT	Round (Daddy)	84-86	6	9, 9	¾	2	-
ARTHUR	Square (Grandad)	39-41	8	11	2	2	-
BRENDA	Square (18) (Cheque)	15-17	8	11	2	2	¼
CAMELLIA	Square	63-65	8	11	2	2	-
DAVID	Square (17)	24-26	8	11	2	2	-
DENIS	Square (15) (Tennis)	66-68	8	11	2	2½	1
DONALD	Square (27) (Cricket)	54-56	8	11	2	3	¼
EDWARD	Square (1) (Teddy)	75-77	8	11	2	2½	-
GARETH	Round (Dad)	18-20	8	11	1½	1½	-
GERALDINE	Horseshoe (Riding)	78-80	10	14	2½	3½	-
JEANETTE	Round	30-32	8	11	1½	2	-
JINA	Round	36-38	6	9	¾	1½	-
KEVIN	Square (Football)	33-35	8	11	2	2	1
LUCY	Figure 3	87-89	Figure 3	13	2	2	¼
MELISSA	Square (Ballet)	21-23	8	11	2	3	¼
NAN	Round (Nan)	90-92	8	11	1½	2	-
NAOMI	Figure 5	81-83	Figure 5	13	1½	2	2
NATALIE	Round	57-59	8	11	1½	1½	-
PAUL	Square (18)	27-29	8	11	2	2	-
RITA	Square	69-71	8	11	2	3	-
ROWENA	Square (15)	48-50	8	11	2	3	-
TRACY	Round (5)	51-53	6	9	¾	2	-
VERONICA	Square (Mother)	45-47	8	11	2	3½	-
VIOLET	Round (Grandma)	60-62	8	11	1½	2½	-
WILLIAM	Square (Book)	93-95	8	14	2	3	-
YVETTE	Round	72-74	8	12	1½	2½	½

This reference table is a guide to the materials used to produce the actual cakes featured in this book. You can, of course, choose whatever material quantities and sizes you wish. Refer to the main photograph in each instance for the appropriate shape of board and cake.

N.B. As you will see in our step-by-step photographs, there are some instances in which we have used coloured Royal Icing instead of white, since this shows the build-up of decorative work more clearly. Naturally, any colour choice is up to you.

Basic Cake Recipe

Imperial/Metric	American
2 oz/57 g plain flour	½ cup all purpose flour
2 oz/57 g brown sugar	⅓ cup brown sugar
2 oz/57 g butter	¼ cup butter
2½ oz/71 g currants	½ cup currants
2½ oz/71 g sultanas	½ cup seedless white raisins
1 oz/28 g seedless raisins	3 tablespoons seedless raisins
1 oz/28 g glacé cherries	3 tablespoons candied cherries
1½ oz/42 g mixed peel	4½ tablespoons candied peel
¾ oz/21 g ground almonds	2½ tablespoons ground almonds
½ fluid oz/2 teaspoons brandy or rum	2 teaspoons brandy or rum
1 large egg	1 large egg
pinch nutmeg	pinch nutmeg
pinch mixed spice	pinch apple pie spice
pinch salt	pinch salt
¼ lemon zest and juice	¼ lemon zest and juice

Preparation. First line your tin with a double layer of buttered greaseproof paper. Then clean and prepare the fruit, halve the cherries. Mix all fruit together with lemon zest. Sift flour, spices and salt.
Method. Beat the butter until light. Add sugar to butter and beat again until light. Gradually add egg, beating in thoroughly after each addition. Stir in ground almonds. Fold in flour and spices. Finally add fruit together with brandy or rum and lemon juice. Mix well together and transfer to tin.

It is most important to follow the exact measurements and mixture of the foregoing ingredients.

In baking the cake initially, if one pint of water is placed in a meat tray in the bottom of the oven, this will create sufficient humidity to keep the top of the cake moist and ensure level results in baking. Remove water after half baking time.

When the cake is baked, leave it in the tin (pan) for one day, remove from tin (pan) then sprinkle the appropriate quantity of soaking mixture. Wrap cake in waxed paper and leave in a cupboard for three weeks. When the waxed paper becomes sticky, this means that moisture is seeping out, a sure sign that the cake is mature. If more liquid is required, add just before marzipanning. A cake needs no more than three weeks to mature.

CAKE PORTIONS: TO CALCULATE SIZE OF FRUIT CAKE REQUIRED 8 PORTIONS ARE GENERALLY CUT FROM EACH 1 LB OF FINISHED ICED CAKE.
Soaking mixture. Equal quantities of Rum, Sherry and Glycerine or spirits of choice. 1 tbls. per 1 lb of cake when required.

Glycerine – Table for use

For soft-cutting icing (per 1 lb or 454 g or 3½ cups of ready-made Royal Icing) use 1 teaspoon of glycerine for the bottom tier of a 3-tier wedding cake.
2 teaspoons of glycerine for the middle tier,
3 teaspoons of glycerine for the top tier,
or for single tier cakes.
(N.B. Glycerine only to be added after Royal Icing has been made.)
NO GLYCERINE IN ROYAL ICING FOR RUNOUTS OR No. 1 WORK.

Royal Icing Recipe

Imperial/Metric
1½ ozs/42 g powdered egg white
½ pint/284 ml cold water
3½ lb/1½ kg best icing sugar sieved
OR
½ oz/14 g powdered egg white
3 fluid ozs/3 tablespoons cold water
1 lb/454 g best icing sugar, sieved
OR
3 egg whites (separated the day before)
1 lb/454 g best icing sugar (approximately) sieved

American
¼ cup powdered egg white + 2 tablespoons
1¼ cups cold water
3½ cups confectioner's sugar sifted
OR
¼ cup powdered egg white
3 tablespoons cold water
3½ cups confectioner's sugar, sifted
OR
3 egg whites (separated the day before)
3½ cups confectioner's sugar (approximately) sifted

Preparation. All equipment used must be perfectly cleaned and sterilised. Pour water into a jug and stir in powdered egg white. This will go lumpy and necessitates standing the mixture for one hour, stirring occasionally. Then strain through a muslin.

Method. Pour solution or egg whites into a mixing bowl and place the icing sugar on top. A drop of blue colour (color) may be added for white icing. Beat on slow speed for approximately 15-20 minutes or until the right consistency is obtained. (If powdered egg white is used the Royal Icing will keep in good condition for 2 weeks. Fresh egg whites will deteriorate quicker). Store Royal Icing in sealed container in a cool place.

Buttercream
(Referred to as CREAM in the Book)

Imperial/Metric
4 ozs/113 g butter
6-8 ozs/170-227 g icing sugar
1-2 tablespoons warm water
essence or flavouring of choice

American
½ cup butter
1⅓-2 cups confectioner's sugar
1-2 tablespoons warm water
extract or flavouring of choice

Method. Sift icing sugar. Soften butter and beat until light. Gradually add the icing sugar beating well after each addition. Add essence (extract) or flavouring (flavoring) of choice and water (carefully).

Heavy Genoese Sponge Recipe

Imperial/Metric
3 oz/85 g butter
3 oz/85 g margarine
6 oz/170 g caster sugar
3 eggs, lightly beaten
6 oz/170 g self-raising flour sieved

American
6 tablespoons butter
6 tablespoons margarine
¾ cup sugar
3 eggs, lightly beaten
1½ cups self-raising flour sifted

Preparation. First line your tin (pans) with greased greaseproof paper.

Method. Cream butter and margarine. Add sugar and beat until light in colour and fluffy in texture. Add the egg a little at a time beating after each addition. Carefully fold in the flour.
Bake: 190°C, 375°F, Gas 5. 20-25 minutes.

½ recipe makes 1 @ 8" Rd sponge	or 1 @ 7" Sq
1 recipe makes 1 @ 10" Rd sponge	or 1 @ 9" Sq
1½ recipe makes 1 @ 12" Rd sponge	or 1 @ 11" Sq

Sugar Paste Recipe (Cold Fondant Recipe)

Imperial/Metric
1 lb/454 g icing sugar, sieved
1 egg white
2 ozs/57 g liquid glucose (Slightly warmed)

American
3½ cups Confectioner's sugar, sifted
1 egg white
4 tablespoons liquid glucose (Slightly warmed)

Method. Add egg white and glucose to icing sugar. Blend all ingredients together. Knead well until a smooth paste is obtained.
Keep in a polythene bag or sealed container and in a cool place. Colour and flavour (flavor) as required.

CONVERSION TABLES

WEIGHT		SIZE	
IMPERIAL	METRIC	IMPERIAL	METRIC
½ oz	14 g	5 ins	12.5 cm
1 oz	28 g	6 ins	15 cm
2 oz	57 g	7 ins	18 cm
3 oz	85 g	8 ins	20.5 cm
4 oz	113 g	9 ins	23 cm
5 oz	142 g	10 ins	25.5 cm
6 oz	170 g	11 ins	28 cm
7 oz	198 g	12 ins	30.5 cm
8 oz	227 g	13 ins	33 cm
9 oz	255 g	14 ins	35.5 cm
10 oz	284 g	15 ins	38 cm
11 oz	312 g	16 ins	40.5 cm
12 oz	340 g		
13 oz	369 g		
14 oz	397 g		
15 oz	425 g		
16 oz	454 g		

	LIQUID	
IMPERIAL	METRIC	AMERICAN
1 tsp.	5 ml	1 tsp
1 tbsp	15 ml	1 tbsp
1 fl.oz	28 ml	⅛ cup
2 fl. oz	57 ml	¼ cup
3 fl. oz	85 ml	⅜ cup
4 fl. oz	113 ml	½ cup
¼ pint	142 ml	⅝ cup
½ pint	284 ml	1¼ cup
1 pint	568 ml	2½ cup

Note: AUSTRALIAN TABLESPOON
4 tsp. 20ml 1 tbsp (AUS)

CAKE SIZES AND QUANTITIES WITH APPROXIMATE BAKING TIMES
(QUANTITIES ARE STATED IN MULTIPLES OF EACH OF THE BASIC RECIPES)

SIZE ins	Basic Fruit Cake Recipe (Bake at 275°F, 140°C, Gas Mark 1)						Heavy Genoese Sponge Recipe (Bake at 375°F, 190°C, Gas Mark 5)			
	ROUND	SQUARE	HORSE SHOE	HEART	HEXAGONAL	APPROX TIMING	ROUND	SQUARE	APPROX TIMING
5	1	1½	-	1½	1	1½-1¾ hrs	-	-	-
6	1½	2	1¼	2	1½	1¾-2 hrs	-	-	-
7	2	3	-	3	2	2½-3 hrs	-	½	20-25 mins
8	3	4	2½	4	3	3½-4 hrs	½	-	20-25 mins
9	4	5	-	5	4	4-4½ hrs	-	1	20-25 mins
10	5	6	4½	6	5	4¼-4¾ hrs	1	-	25-30 mins
11	6	7	-	7	6	4½-5 hrs	-	1½	25-30 mins
12	7	8	6½	8	7	5-5½ hrs	1½	-	25-30 mins

Template graph and instructions.

(Do not remove or draw directly onto this graph.)

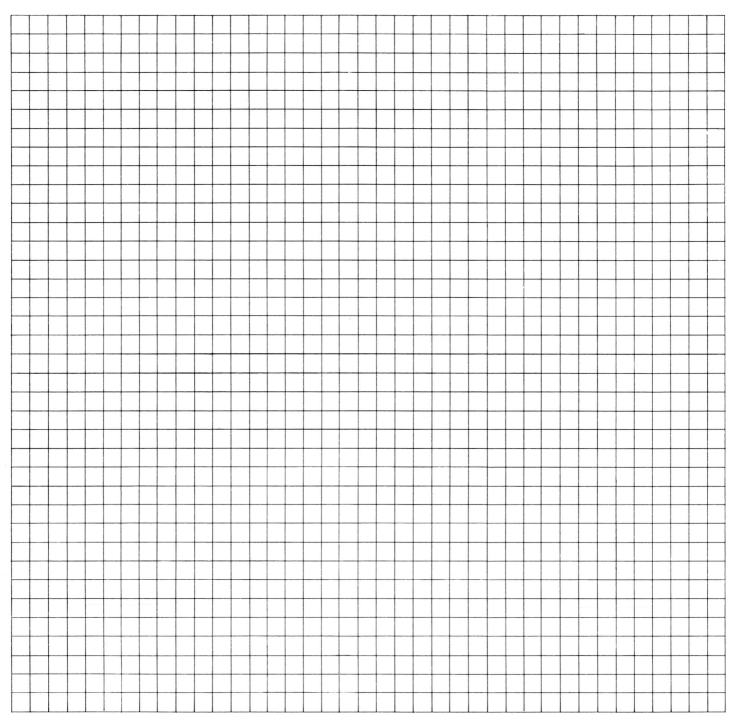

Explanatory note:
Most cakes in this book include artwork necessitating the use of graphs (for an example please refer to the drawing of the racket template in picture No.2 of the cake 'Denis' on page 67). All graphs, such as that in picture No.2, need to be adjusted to obtain the correct scale. This can be achieved by using the following instructions.

Instructions:
1. Count and record the number of squares in picture No.2.
2. Cover the TEMPLATE GRAPH with a sheet of greaseproof paper and count out, mark and trace the equivalent number of squares on the greaseproof paper.
3. Remove the greaseproof paper graph and return to page 67.
4. Wherever the drawing in picture No.2 crosses a line, mark the identical crossing point on the greaseproof paper graph.
5. Still using the picture as a guide, join the marks on the greaseproof paper graph to re-create drawing No.2 on page 67.

Equipment.

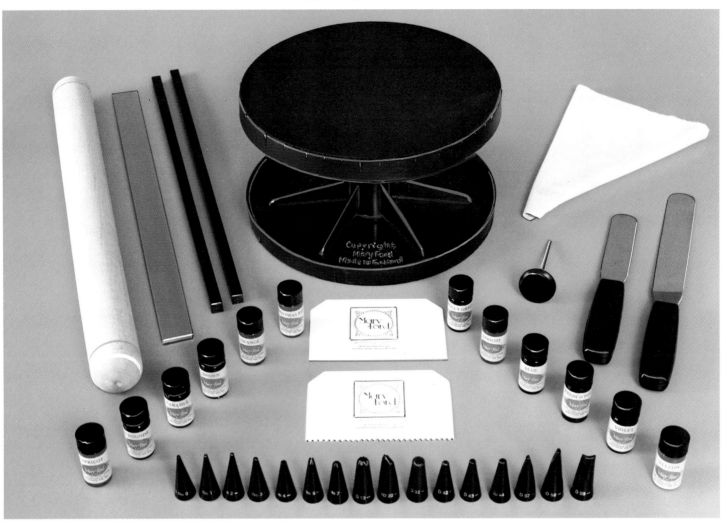

Turntable	Straight edge	Plain scraper	Flower nail
6″ Palette knife	Rolling pin	Serrated scraper	Edible colourings
4″ Palette knife	Pair of marzipan spacers	Nylon piping bag	Icing tubes

The above are the items of equipment used in making the cakes that appear in our book. Most of them were designed by us, and they are all obtainable through the Company's Mail Order Department.

You will find each item, and many more, featured in our catalogue, which can be obtained from:

Mary Ford Cake Artistry Centre Ltd.
28–30 Southbourne Grove, Southbourne,
Bournemouth BH6 3RA.

**Cake decorating courses are held at the Mary Ford Centre.
For further details please apply to the above address**

Mary Ford Tube No.'s showing their shapes.

0   1   2   3   4   5   6   7   13   22   32   42   43   44   57   58   59

The above are all the icing tubes used in this book.
Please note that these are Mary Ford tubes, but comparable tubes may be used.

Piped Designs.

1. 1st stage of 6-dot sequence, pipe 3 dots.
2. 2nd stage, pipe 2 further dots.
3. 3rd stage, pipe last dot to complete sequence.
4. Graduated bulbs.
5. Shell.
6. Cone-shaped shell.
7. Rosette.
8. 'C' line.
9. Bold 'C'.
10. 'S' line.
11. Rope.
12. Curved rope.
13. Spiral shell.
14. 'C' scroll.
15. 'S' scroll.
16. Left-to-right scroll.
17. Right-to-left scroll.

Various Writing Styles.

ABCDEFGHIJKLMNOPQRSTUVWXYZ ÆØ 1234567890

ABCDEFGHIJKLMNOPQRSTUVWXYZ ÆØ 1234567890

A ABCDEFGHIJKLMNOPQRRSTTUVWXYZ

ABCDEEFGHIJKLLMNOPQRSTUVWXYZ 12345678890

ABCDEFGHIJKLMNOPQRSTUVWXYZ 1234567890

ABCDEFGHIJKLMNOPQRSTUVWXYZ 1234567890

ABCDEFGHIJKLMNOPQRSTUVWXYZ ÆØ 1234567890

ABCDEFGHIJKLMNOPQRSTUVWXYZ

ABCDEFGHIJKLMNOPQRSTUVWXYZ 1234567890

ABCDEFGHIJKLMNOPQRSTUVWXYZ 1234567890

ABCDEFGHIJKLMNOPQRSTUVWXYZ 1234567890

ABCDEFGHIJKLMNOPQRSTUVWXYZ

Making and filling a greaseproof piping bag

1. A sheet of greaseproof paper – 12″×8″ – required.

2. Cut sheet diagonally as shown.

3. Turn one triangle to position shown.

4. Fold paper from right to centre.

5. Lift corner from left to right.

6. Fold under and pull into shape.

7. Fold in loose ends and cut section. Fold back to secure.

8. Cut off tip of bag and drop in tube.

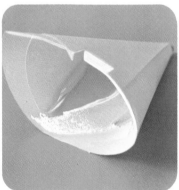

9. Using a palette knife, half fill bag with Royal Icing.

10. Carefully fold and roll the open end to seal bag, which is then ready for use.

11. To make a LEAF BAG repeat 1–7 and then flatten tip.

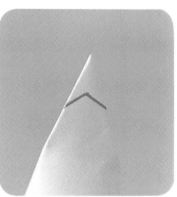

12. Picture showing shape of tip to be cut.

13. Now cut tip.

14. For using TWO COLOURS partially fill one side of bag with one colour.

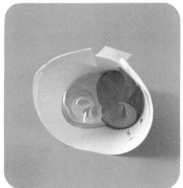

15. Fill remaining half with 2nd colour. Repeat 10.

16. Picture showing effect of using two colours of Royal Icing.

How to marzipan

17. Picture showing a matured fruit cake with lining paper removed.

18. Upturn cake, place on board (3″ larger) and if required brush on spirits and glycerine.

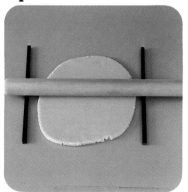

19. Using icing sugar for dusting, roll marzipan between spacers (approx: ⅜″ thick), as shown.

20. Cut marzipan to size using the cake tin (in which the cake was baked) as guide.

21. After removing surplus marzipan brush off any loose icing sugar.

22. Jam the marzipan with boiling apricot puree by applying it with a palette knife.

23. Lay cake onto the jammed marzipan.

24. Upturn cake and replace on board.

25. Picture showing a square cake (which is prepared in the same way as a round cake).

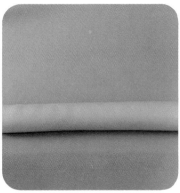

26. Form remaining marzipan into a sausage shape.

27. Now roll the marzipan into a thin strip (wide enough to cover the cake side).

28. Cut marzipan for side (length=approx: 3 times diameter) and then jam as in 22.

29. Fix marzipan to cake side and trim off surplus (L.D. approx: 3 days).

30. For a square cake roll out a sheet of marzipan to cover the 4 sides.

31. Cut the sheet into 4 separate strips to fit sides.

32. Jam and fix each strip then trim (L.D. approx: 3 days).

HOW TO CUT A WEDGE
33. After marzipanning, cut wedge from cake, as shown.

34. Replace wedge.

35. Mark board to show position of wedge. Place cake on turntable.

HOW TO COAT A CAKE
36. Spread Royal Icing around side of cake with a palette knife.

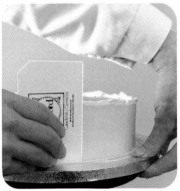

37. Place hands in position shown (holding the scraper against the cake side).

38. Holding scraper steady with one hand, revolve the turntable one complete turn with the other hand.

39. Repeat 36–38 until side is smooth.

40. Using the palette knife, remove surplus icing fom cake.

41. Immediately remove wedge.

42. Clean sides of wedge and replace (L.D. 12 hrs).

43. Using the palette knife, place Royal Icing on top of the cake.

44. Using the palette knife in a paddling movement, spread the icing evenly over the cake top.

45. Using a stainless steel rule, start to level the icing.

46. Continue to use the rule in a backwards and forwards motion to level icing.

47. Picture showing coated cake.

48. Remove surplus icing from edges of cake top and wedge (L.D. 12 hrs). Repeat 36–48 twice more.

11

49. 1½ yards of satin ribbon on a piece of greaseproof paper – approx: 8″×6″ required.

50. Fold the paper over the centre of the ribbon.

51. Fold the paper and ribbon in half and place to wedge.

52. Replace wedge.

53. Roll up equal lengths of ribbon ends and fix to side of cake.

HOW TO COAT A BOARD.
54. Picture showing hands and scraper in readiness to coat board.

55. Holding scraper steady in one hand, revolve the turntable one complete turn with the other (see picture 38).

56. For coating a square (or hexagonal, etc.) cake, coat the opposite sides (L.D. 12 hrs).

57. Now coat remaining sides (L.D. 12 hrs).

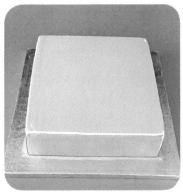

58. Coat the top as for round cake (L.D. 12 hrs). Repeat 56–58 twice more.

HOW TO MAKE A SUGAR PASTE ROSE BUD.
59. Roll a piece of sugar paste into the shape shown.

60. Flatten back to form sharp edge.

61. Roll up the sugar paste as shown.

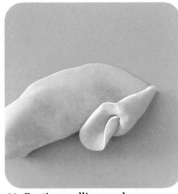

62. Continue rolling, as shown.

63. Fold over remaining sugar paste.

64. Remove surplus sugar paste, then bend back edge to form bud.

HOW TO MAKE A SUGAR PASTE ROSE.
65. Repeat 59–64 but finishing with bud in upright position.

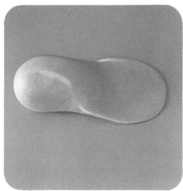

66. Roll out sugar paste and flatten one end.

67. Cut away surplus leaving the petal.

68. Wrap petal around the bud and slightly dampen with water to fix.

69. Repeat 66–68 for the second petal.

70. Repeat 66–68 making and fixing larger petals until size of rose required is obtained.

MAKING ROYAL ICING BIRDS.
71. Pipe wings on waxed paper, working from left to right (No.1) (L.D. 12 hrs).

72. Pipe tail on waxed paper (two types shown) (No.1).

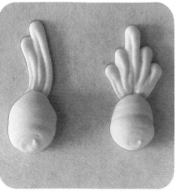

73. Pipe body against tail (No.1).

74. Lifting icing bag pipe neck, head and beak (No.1).

75. Immediately fix wings to body (L.D. 12 hrs).

MAKING SUGAR BELLS
76. Pipe a bulb on waxed paper (No.3).

77. Pipe a second bulb on top (No.3).

78. Sprinkle granulated sugar over the bulbs (then leave until outside of bulbs are dry).

79. Scoop out unset Royal Icing from centre of bell.

80. Pipe-in hammer (No.1).

13

PIPING SUGAR FLOWERS & ROSES

PIPING SUGAR FLOWERS
81. Picture showing items required=flower nail, waxed paper and piping bag with petal tube (No.58).

82. Fix a square of waxed paper to top of flower nail and hold in position shown.

83. Keeping thick end of tube to the centre of flower, pipe 1st petal.

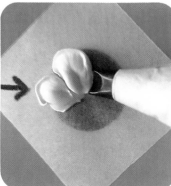

84. Turn nail and pipe next petal.

85. Turn nail and pipe 3rd petal.

86. Turn nail and pipe 4th petal.

87. Turn nail and pipe 5th petal.

88. Turn nail and pipe the last petal.

89. Picture showing the piped petals.

90. Pipe a centre bulb (No.2) (L.D. 24 hrs).

PIPING SUGAR ROSES
91. Form a cone of marzipan.

92. Using stiff Royal Icing, pipe the centre of the rose (No.57).

93. Pipe a petal behind the centre (No.57).

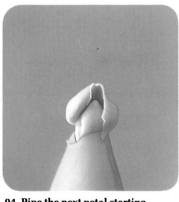

94. Pipe the next petal starting inside the 1st petal (No.57).

95. Pipe the 3rd petal, starting inside the 2nd petal and ending over part of the 1st petal (No.57) (L.D. 15 m).

96. Repeat 93–95 for 5 petals around outside of rose (L.D. 24 hrs). Remove from cone.

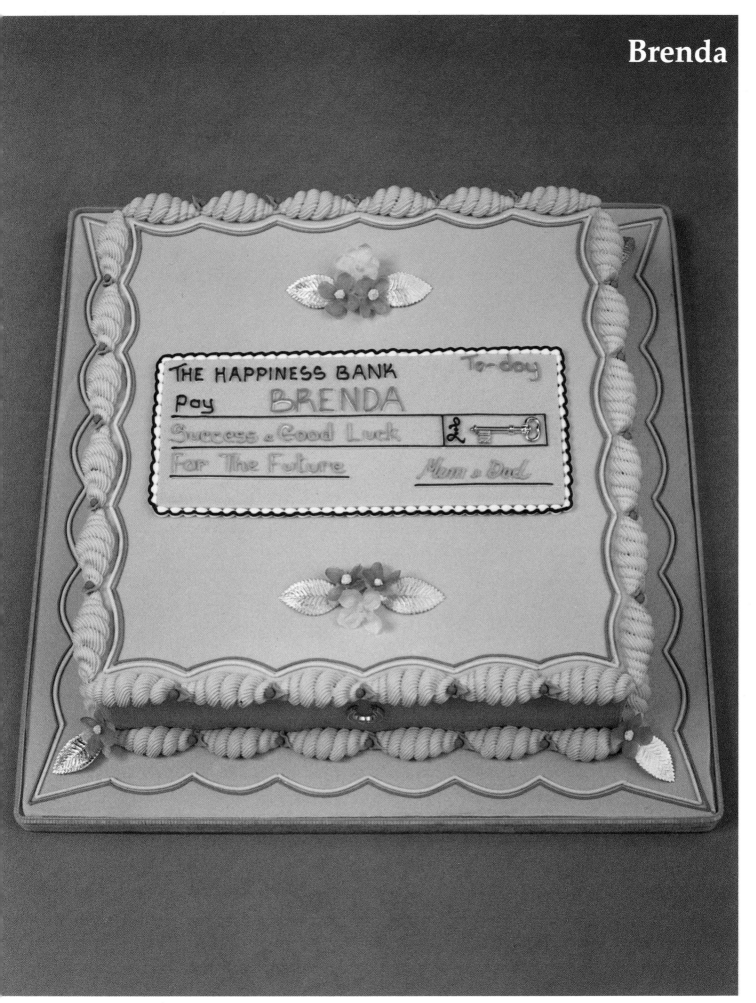

THE HAPPINESS BANK — To-day
Pay BRENDA
Success & Good Luck
For The Future — Mum & Dad

NOTE: *Before attempting to decorate this cake, please study the whole sequence of photographs and notes and ensure you have the proper equipment and materials, as well as sufficient time. Additional information can be found on pages 4-14 and 96.*

1. Roll out and cut a sheet of sugar paste – 2½″ × 6½″ – to form cheque.

2. Fix cheque to centre of cake, as shown.

3. Pipe shells around edge of cheque (No.2).

4. Pipe a line over each shell (No.1).

5. Pipe title of Bank (No.1).

6. Pipe 'To-day' (No.1).

7. Pipe lines on cheque, as shown (No.1).

8. Pipe 'Pay' and name of choice (No.1).

9. Pipe message of choice (No.1).

10. Pipe further message of choice (No.1).

11. Pipe signature of choice (No.1).

12. Overpipe, as shown (No.0).

13. Overpipe, as shown (No.0).

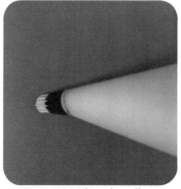

14. How to pipe a barrel scroll. Step 1 = Hold bag at angle shown (No.44).

15. Step 2 = Start piping a barrel rope in a clockwise rotating motion.

16. Step 3=Continue piping barrel scroll, as shown.

NOTE: Before attempting to decorate this cake, please study the whole sequence of photographs and notes and ensure you have the proper equipment and materials, as well as sufficient time. Additional information can be found on pages 4-14 and 96.

17. Step 4 = Continue piping barrel scroll, as shown.

18. Picture showing completed barrel scroll.

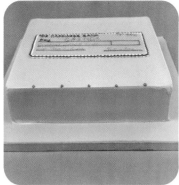

19. Divide cake-top edge into 6 equal portions with piped dots.

20. Pipe a barrel scroll in first portion (No.44).

21. Pipe a barrel scroll in each cake-top portion, as shown (No.44).

22. Repeat 19-21 around remaining cake-top edges.

23. Repeat 19-20 at cake base.

24. Continue piping barrel scrolls around cake base (No.44).

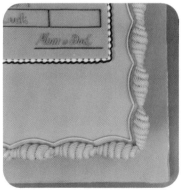

25. Pipe a line beside each cake-top scroll (No.2).

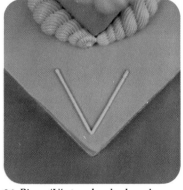

26. Pipe a 'V' at each cake-board corner (No.2).

27. Pipe curved lines around cake-board, as shown (No.2).

28. Pipe inside each cake-top No.2 line (No.1).

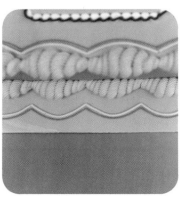

29. Pipe outside each cake-board No.2 line (No.1).

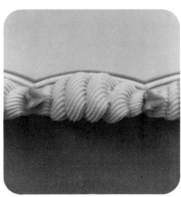

30. Pipe a leaf between each barrel scroll (Leaf bag).

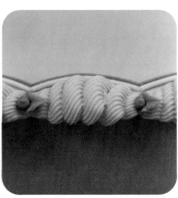

31. Pipe a bulb to each leaf (No.1).

32. Pipe '£' (No.1) then fix an artificial key and decorate as required.

Gareth

1. Use serrated scraper on cake-side to complete icing.

2. Dab Royal Icing on cake-top with palette knife.

3. Spread icing with palette knife to form part of cloud.

4. Repeat 2 and 3, as shown.

5. Hold piping bag in position shown at cake-top edge (No.13).

6. Begin piping rosette.

7. Complete rosette circle.

8. Picture showing complete rosette.

9. Repeat 5 to 7, as shown.

10. Continue piping rosettes around cake-top, but leave four rosette spaces, as shown.

11. Mark and pipe-in the four remaining rosettes (No.13).

12. Pipe rosette at cake-base (No.13).

13. Pipe a second rosette, as shown.

14. Repeat 10 at base.

15. Repeat 11 at base.

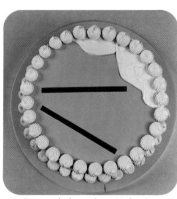

16. Cut guide lines (see 'Helen') and place on cake-top as shown.

17. Pipe 'To', as shown (No.2).

18. Pipe 'D' as shown (No.2).

19. Pipe 'a' as shown (No.2).

20. Pipe 'd' as shown (No.2).

21. Picture showing inscription.

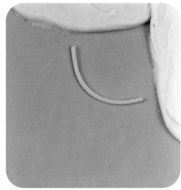

22. Pipe curved line to give sun effect (No.2).

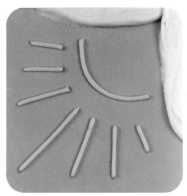

23. Pipe sun rays (No.2).

24. Pipe curved rope in position shown on cake-top (No.2).

25. Continue piping rope from cloud to cloud, as shown (No.2).

26. Pipe curved rope in position shown on cake-board (No.2).

27. Continue piping rope around cake-board, as shown (No.2).

28. Pipe large dot in centre of one cake-top rosette (No.2).

29. Pipe a large dot in each rosette (No.2).

30. Pipe a line beside the 'T' and 'D' (No.1).

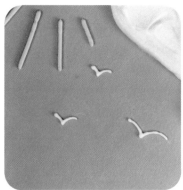

31. Pipe bird motifs, as shown (No.1).

32. Fix ribbon and decorations of choice.

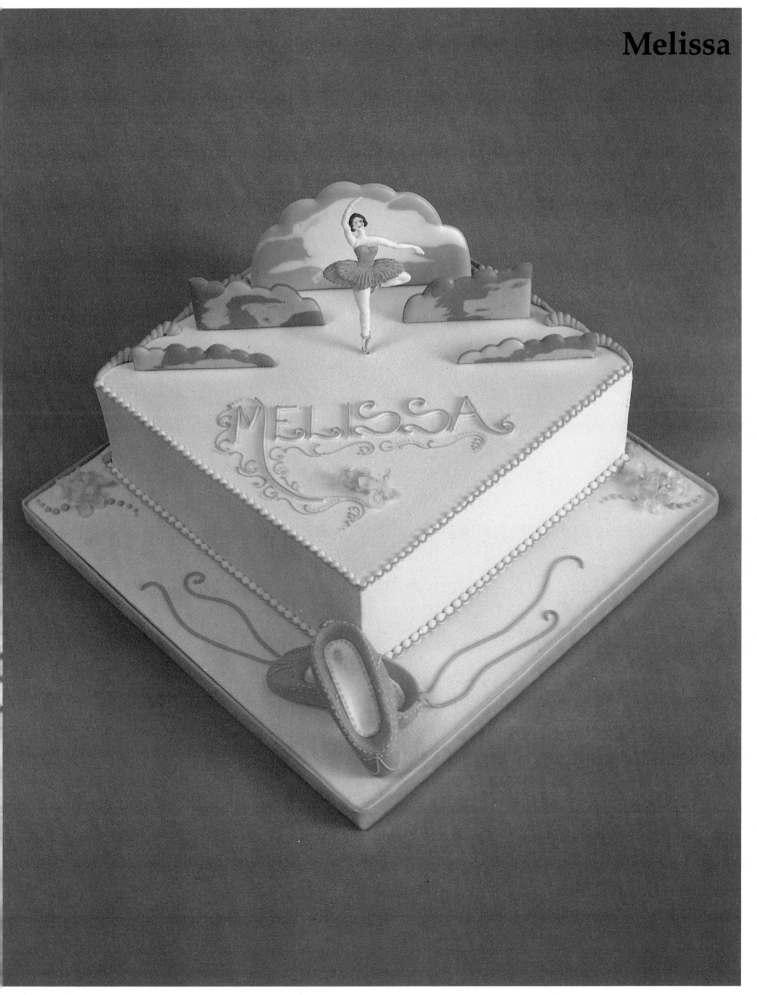

NOTE: Before attempting to decorate this cake, please study the whole sequence of photographs and notes and ensure you have the proper equipment and materials, as well as sufficient time. Additional information can be found on pages 4-14 and 96.

1. Drawing showing template of ballerina.

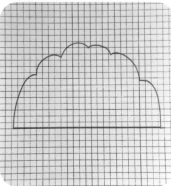

2. Drawing showing template of cloud.

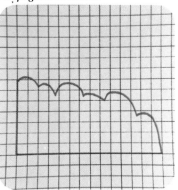

3. Drawing showing template of high stage scenery.

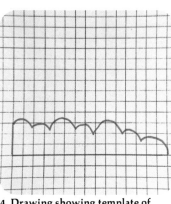

4. Drawing showing template of low stage scenery.

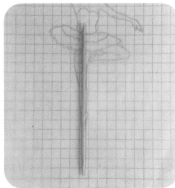

5. Place cocktail stick on waxed paper in position shown.

6. Pipe the parts of the ballerina shown (No.1).

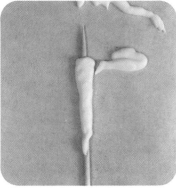

7. Pipe over the cocktail stick, as shown (No.1).

8. Pipe remaining parts of ballerina (No.1) (L.D. 24 hrs).

9. Remove ballerina from waxed paper and pipe reverse side, as shown (No.1) (L.D. 24 hrs).

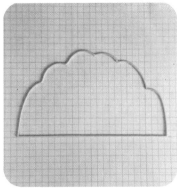

10. Outline cloud on waxed paper (No.2).

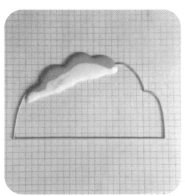

11. Flood-in the part of the cloud shown in the colours shown.

12. Immediately continue flooding-in the part of the cloud shown.

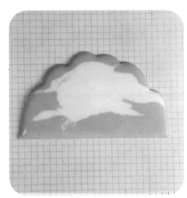

13. Immediately continue flooding-in the part of the cloud shown to complete cloud (L.D. 24 hrs).

14. Outline and flood-in the stage scenery in the colours shown on waxed paper (L.D. 24 hrs).

15. Repeat 14 in opposite direction.

16. Position coated cake on cakeboard, as shown.

22

17. Mould sugar paste to shape shown to form ballet shoe (2 required).

18. Fix thin strip of sugar paste to inside of each ballet shoe.

19. Decorate each shoe, as shown (No.1).

20. Fix cloud to cake-top in position shown.

21. Fix scenery to cake-top in position shown.

22. Make a small hole in cake-top and then fix ballerina in position shown.

23. Pipe shells along the back of the cloud and scenery, as shown (No.43).

24. Pipe a pair of 'S' scrolls on the cake-top edge shown (No.44).

25. Complete each 'S' scroll cake-top edge with 'C' scrolls (No. 43).

26. Pipe shells beneath cake-top scrolls at cake-base (No.44) and (No.43).

27. Pipe inscription of choice (No.2) and then overpipe inscription (No.1).

28. Decorate inscription, as shown (No.1) and fix flowers of choice to cake-top.

29. Pipe shells along remaining cake-top edges and cake-base (No.2) then pipe a line over each shell (No.1).

30. Fix ballet shoes on cake-board, as shown.

31. Pipe ballet shoe ties, as shown (No.2).

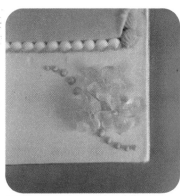

32. Fix matching artificial flowers and pipe graduated dots on cake-board (No.1).

David

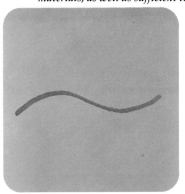

1. Pictures 1-5 show how to practice piping an 'S' scroll. Step No.1 = Draw curved line on ceramic tile.

2. Step 2 = Start piping a rope over the curved line in a clock-wise rotating motion (No.7).

3. Step 3 = Continue piping the rope over the curved line to position shown.

4. Step 4 = Continue piping rope over the curved line but in a gradually reduced size, as shown.

5. Step 5 = Complete the scroll by piping the tail (sliding the tube to the end of the curved line and reducing pressure).

6. Picture showing completed 'S' scroll.

7. Pictures 7-11 show how to practice piping a 'C' scroll. Step No.1 = Draw curved line on ceramic tile.

8. Step 2 = Start piping a rope over the curved line in a clock-wise rotating motion (No.7).

9. Step 3 = Continue piping the rope over the curved line to position shown.

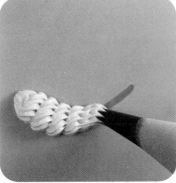

10. Step 4 = Continue piping rope over the curved line but in a gradually reduced size, as shown.

11. Step 5 = Complete the scroll by piping the tail (sliding the tube to the end of the curved line and reducing pressure).

12. Picture showing combination of 'S' and 'C' scrolls.

13. Pictures 13-15 show how to practice piping 'S' and 'C' scrolls in opposite direction. Step 1 = Draw curved lines on ceramic tile.

14. Step 2 = Repeat 2-5 but in an anti-clockwise rotating motion and starting from the right.

15. Step 3 = Repeat 8-11 but in an anti-clockwise rotating motion and starting from the right.

16. Picture showing a series of linked 'S' scrolls.

NOTE: *Before attempting to decorate this cake, please study the whole sequence of photographs and notes and ensure you have the proper equipment and materials, as well as sufficient time. Additional information can be found on pages 4-14 and 96.*

17. Pipe a left-to-right 'S' scroll on cake-top edge, as shown (No.7).

18. Pipe a joining 'C' scroll, as shown (No.7).

19. Pipe a right-to-left 'C' scroll on cake-top edge, as shown (No.7).

20. Pipe a joining 'C' scroll, as shown (No.7).

21. Repeat 17-20 around cake-top, as shown.

22. Pipe a line around cake base (No.7) (L.D.30m).

23. Pipe an 'S' scroll at cake-base corner, as shown (No.7).

24. Continue piping 'S' scrolls around cake-base and at each corner, as shown (No.7).

25. Picture showing cake so far.

26. Pipe a line inside each cake-top scroll (No.3).

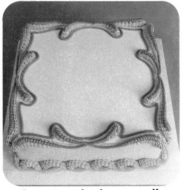

27. Overpipe each cake-top scroll (No.3).

28. Overpipe each cake-base scroll (No.3).

29. Overpipe each cake-top scroll (No.2).

30. Overpipe each cake-base scroll (No.2).

31. Pipe inscription of choice to cake-top (No.2) then overpipe inscription (No.1).

32. Pipe lines under inscription, as shown (No.1). Fix decorations of choice.

1. Prepare 8″ square cake on 11″ square board, using combed scraper for sides.

2. Cut out a paper template 6½″ × 6½″.

3. Fold template in half.

4. Fold template in half again.

5. Fold folded template diagonally.

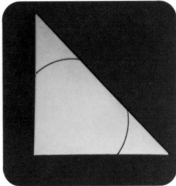

6. Draw and then cut the two curved lines shown.

7. Unfold template and place on cake-top.

8. Pipe lines inside template (No.2) and outside template (No.4).

9. Pipe a line inside the No.4 line and then overpipe the No.4 line (No.3).

10. Pipe a line inside the No.3 line and then overpipe the No.3 lines (No.2).

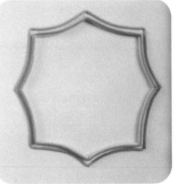

11. Pipe a line outside the inner pattern No.2 line (No.1) and then overpipe the No.2 line (No.1).

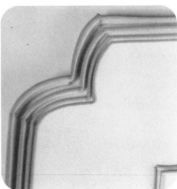

12. Pipe a line inside the No:2 line (No.1) and then overpipe the No.2 lines (No.1).

13. Pipe inscription of choice in central cake-top pattern (No.2).

14. Overpipe the inscription (No.1).

15. Overpipe the inscription (No.0).

16. Overpipe the inside No.1 line (No.0).

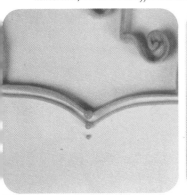

17. Pipe 3 graduated dots at each of the points of the inner pattern shown (No. 1).

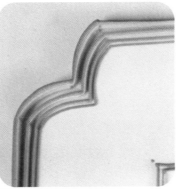

18. Overpipe outer No. 1 line (No. 0).

19. Pipe a line each side of the inscription (No. 2).

20. Pipe a line beside each inscription No. 2 line (No. 1) and overpipe each No. 2 line (No. 1).

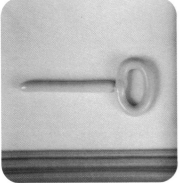

21. Pipe first section of keys in positions shown on cake-top (No. 3).

22. Complete key shapes (No. 3).

23. Pipe figures '18' in positions shown on cake-top (No. 2).

24. Complete '18' motifs, as shown (No. 1).

25. Pipe shells around cake-top and cake-base edges (No. 6).

26. Pipe a line across each cake-board corner (No. 4).

27. Pipe a line beside each cake-board No. 4 line (No. 3) and then overpipe each No. 4 line (No. 3).

28. Follow sequence in 10, 12 & 18 on each cake-board corner.

29. Pipe 'S' and lines on each cake-board side, as shown (No. 2).

30. Pipe 'S' bulbs and pipe lines beside No. 2 lines (No. 1) and overpipe the No. 2 lines (No. 1).

31. Fix artificial horseshoe to each cake-top corner with decorated bulb (No. 1).

32. Pipe graduated bulbs and decorate each cake-board corner (No. 1).

1. One plain plastic scraper required.

2. Cut a 'V' into the scraper at half the height of the cake.

3. Coat cake and board in normal way using the scraper to form a central band around the cake side.

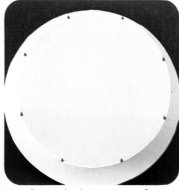

4. Mark top of cake into 8 equal divisions with piped dots, as shown.

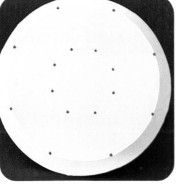

5. Mark inner top of cake into 8 equal divisions (in line with outer marks) with a dot, as shown.

6. Pipe a curved line between each pair of inner dots, as shown (No.3).

7. Pipe a line each side of each No.3 line (No.2).

8. Overpipe each No.3 line (No.2).

9. Pipe a line inside each inner No.2 line and outside each outer No.2 line (No.1).

10. Overpipe each No.2 line (No.1).

11. Pipe a spiral shell on cake-top edge (No.42).

12. Pipe a larger spiral shell on cake-top edge (No.44).

13. Pipe a spiral shell on cake-top edge (No.42). (Note: The 3 shells to lie between a pair of dots).

14. Repeat 11–13 between each pair of outer edge dots.

15. Repeat 11–13 around base of cake.

16. Pipe curved lines around cake top and board, as shown (No.2).

17. Pipe a line beside each of the No.2 lines piped in 16 (No.1) and then overpipe each of the No.2 lines (No.1).

18. Pipe an octagonal line on the cake top, as shown (No.2).

19. Pipe a line beside the No.2 octagonal line (No.1) and then overpipe the No.2 line (No.1).

20. Pipe a wavy line on the cake top, as shown (No.2).

21. Pipe leaves on the wavy line using two colours of Royal Icing from a leaf bag.

22. Pipe a broken wavy line around the side of the cake, as shown (No.2) (T as necessary).

23. Repeat 21 around cake side.

24. Pipe curved lines on each large spiral shell, as shown (No.3).

25. Overpipe each No.3 line (No.2).

26. Overpipe each No.2 line (No.1).

27. Pipe loops on the cake top, as shown (No.2) then overpipe (No.1).

28. Flood-in each loop.

29. Pipe a dot against each loop (No.1).

30. Pipe scallops against each large curved base line (No.1).

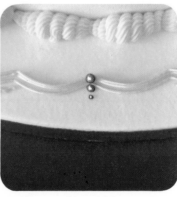

31. Pipe 3 graduated dots at each small curved base line division (No.1).

32. Fix candle-holders and candles on cake top and ribbon to board edge.

1. Pipe two straight lines across the top of the cake in the positions shown (No.2).

2. Pipe a connecting line across the centre of the cake top, as shown (No.2).

3. Pipe further lines in the positions shown (No.2).

4. Pipe further lines in the positions shown (No.2).

5. Pipe further lines to complete a football field (No.2).

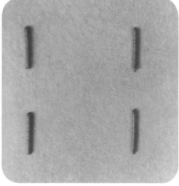

6. Pipe 4 × ½″ high flag posts on waxed paper, as shown (No.2) (L.D. 20 m).

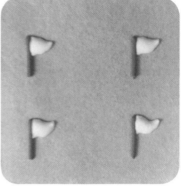

7. Pipe-in a flag on each post (No.2) (L.D. 12 hrs).

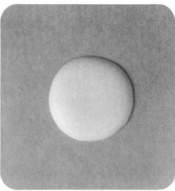

8. Outline and flood-in on waxed paper a 1″ diameter disc (L.D. 24 hrs) (4 required).

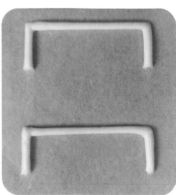

9. Pipe goal posts on waxed paper, as shown (No.4) (L.D. 12 hrs).

10. Paint lines on discs with edible colouring to represent footballs.

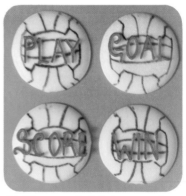

11. Pipe a word of choice on each football (No.1).

12. Form 2″ (approx) diameter sugar paste ball (L.D. 12 hrs).

13. Form two balls of sugar paste.

14. Now mould balls into shape shown.

15. Shape into soccer boots, as shown.

16. Cut boot tops and pierce boot eyes, as shown.

17. Pipe lines on boots, as shown (No.1).

18. Pipe further lines on boots, as shown (No.1).

19. Pipe laces, as shown (No.1) (L.D. 12 hrs).

20. Pipe bulbs on waxed paper to form boot studs (No.2) (L.D. 12 hrs).

21. Fix studs to boot soles, as shown.

22. Pipe lines on the football in the positions shown (No.1) (L.D. 12 hrs).

23. Pipe shells around base of the cake (No.44).

24. Pipe shells along the parts of the cake-top edge shown (No.43).

25. Overpipe base shells with a line (No.3).

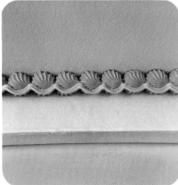

26. Overpipe the No.3 line (No.2).

27. Overpipe the No.2 line (No.1).

28. Pipe message of choice on cake top, as shown (No.1).

29. Pipe a line at each board corner (No.2) and then pipe a line beside each No.2 line (No.1).

30. Fix ball and boots to cake top.

31. Fix goal and flag posts and pipe penalty spots on cake top (No.2).

32. Fix a football disc to each side of the cake and ribbon around board edge.

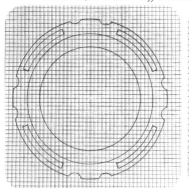

1. Drawing showing template of cake-top and base runouts.

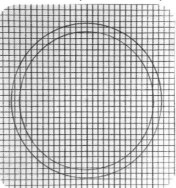

2. Drawing showing template of cake-top ring runout.

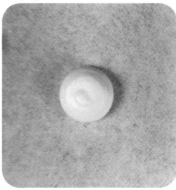

3. To make flowers, pipe bulb on waxed paper (No. 2) (8 required).

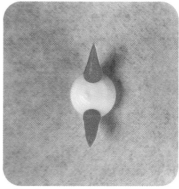

4. Pipe two spikes at angle shown on each bulb (No. 1).

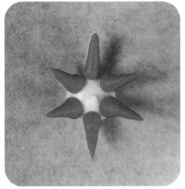

5. Pipe further spikes on each bulb, as shown (No. 1) to complete flowers (L.D. 24 hrs).

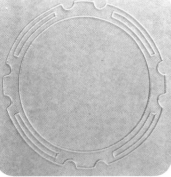

6. Outline the cake-base runout on waxed paper, as shown (No. 1).

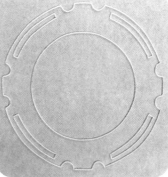

7. Outline the cake-top runout on waxed paper, as shown (No. 1).

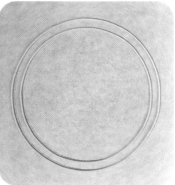

8. Outline ring on waxed paper (No. 1).

9. Flood-in the cake top and base runouts (L.D. 24 hrs).

10. Flood-in the ring (L.D. 24 hrs).

11. Pipe single dots on inner edge of cake-top runout (No. 0).

12. Pipe single dots inside and outside the ring (No. 0) (L.D. 12 hrs).

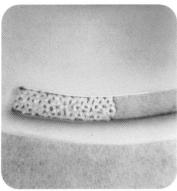

13. Filigree open sections on cake-top and base runouts (No. 0).

14. Pipe 6-dot sequence along each outer edge of the cake-top and base runouts (excluding each half-circle) (No. 0).

15. Pipe single dots in each cake-top and base half-circle of runouts (No. 0) (L.D. 12 hrs).

16. Pipe a line around cake base (No. 3) (L.D. 1 hr).

17. Overpipe the No. 3 line (No. 2) and carefully lower and fix cake-base runout.

18. Pipe a line around cake-top edge (No. 3) (L.D. 1 hr).

19. Pipe bulbs around cake-base, as shown (No. 2).

20. Overpipe the No. 3 line (No. 2) and immediately fix cake-top runout.

21. Pipe bulbs under cake-top runout (No. 3) (T).

22. Pipe a line on inside edge of cake-top runout (No. 2) (L.D. 1 hr).

23. Overpipe the No. 2 line (No. 2) and immediately fix the ring.

24. Pipe scrolled top of 'J', as shown (No. 2).

25. Pipe complete inscription (No. 2).

26. Pipe additional curved lines, as shown (No. 2).

27. Overpipe scrolled lines (No. 1) and then pipe tiny leaves (leaf bag) as shown.

28. Overpipe inscription, as shown (No. 1).

29. Fix a flower in each of the positions indicated.

30. Pipe a line beside the base runout, as shown (No. 2).

31. Pipe further lines in positions indicated on cake-board (No. 1).

32. Pipe single dots in cake-board half-circles (No. 1).

1. Make a triangular template out of card, as shown.

2. Pipe a line each side of the template (No.3).

3. Continue piping the lines vertically down the side of the cake (No.3) (T).

4. Continue piping the lines across the board (No.3).

5. Pipe a line outside each No.3 line (No.2) (T as necessary).

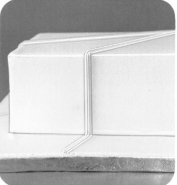

6. Overpipe each No.3 line (No.2) (T as necessary).

7. Pipe a line beside each No.2 line (No.1) (T as necessary).

8. Overpipe each No.2 line (No.1) (T as necessary).

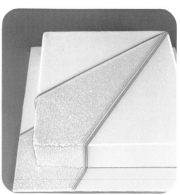

9. Filigree inside the triangular pattern (No.1) (T as necessary).

10. Pipe an 'S' scroll at the side of the cake-top corner shown (No.43).

11. Pipe an 'S' scroll at the side of the cake-top corner shown (No.43).

12. Pipe a 'C' scroll in the position shown (No.43).

13. Pipe a further 'C' scroll, as shown (No.43).

14. Pipe 4 more 'C' scrolls, as shown (No.43).

15. Pipe 4 more 'C' scrolls, as shown (No.43).

16. Pipe shells along top edge shown (No.43).

40

17. Pipe shells along the top edge shown (No.43).

18. Pipe a line along two sides of the base of the cake (beneath the scrolls) (No.43).

19. Pipe matching scrolls along the base of the cake shown (No.43).

20. Pipe matching scrolls along the base of the cake shown (No.43).

21. Pipe matching shells along the base of the cake shown (No.43).

22. Overpipe each scroll (No.3).

23. Pipe a line inside each cake-top 'C' scroll (No.2).

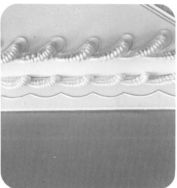

24. Pipe curved lines around board, as shown (No.2).

25. Overpipe each No.3 scroll with a wavy line (No.57).

26. Pipe a dot between each shell (No.1).

27. Pipe a word of choice on the part of the cake top shown (No.2).

28. Pipe a word of choice on the part of the cake top shown (No.2).

29. Pipe a word of choice on the part of the cake top shown (No.3).

30. Overpipe each word (No.1).

31. Fix artificial flowers of choice and leaves to corner.

32. Fix ribbon of choice around the middle and board-edge of cake.

41

1. Drawing showing template of champagne bottle and cork.

2. Drawing showing template of champagne glass.

3. Outline and flood-in on waxed paper the part of the champagne bottle shown (L.D. 15m).

4. Outline and flood-in the part of the champagne glass shown on waxed paper (L.D. 15m).

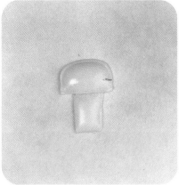

5. Outline and flood-in on waxed paper the champagne cork (L.D. 24 hrs).

6. Flood-in remaining part of the champagne bottle (L.D. 24 hrs).

7. Flood-in remaining part of the champagne glass (L.D. 24 hrs).

8. Paint the cork with edible food colouring.

9. Pipe label lines on champagne bottle, as indicated (No.1).

10. Flood-in labels, as shown (L.D. 2 hrs).

11. Pipe the champagne glass rim (No. 1).

12. Decorate the labels, as shown (No.0).

13. Paint the champagne glass with edible food colouring.

14. Fix champagne bottle, glass and cork to cake-top.

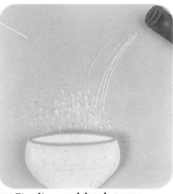

15. Pipe lines and dots between bottle and glass (No.1) then immediately sprinkle granulated sugar over area shown.

16. Pipe inscription of choice on cake-top (No.1) then overpipe inscription (No.1).

17. Pipe curved lines, as shown (No.0).

18. Pipe a right-to-left 'S' scroll at the cake-top corner (No.43).

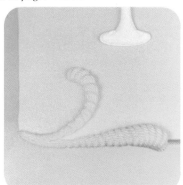

19. Pipe a 'C' scroll, as shown (No.43).

20. Pipe a further 'C' scroll, as shown (No.43).

21. Pipe an 'S' scroll as shown (No. 43).

22. Pipe further 'C' scrolls, as shown (No. 43).

23. Pipe shells around remaining part of cake-top edge (No. 43).

24. Pipe shells around cake-base (No.43).

25. Overpipe each scroll (No.3).

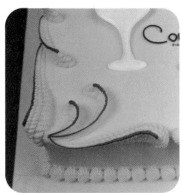

26. Overpipe each scroll (No.2) then overpipe each scroll (No.1).

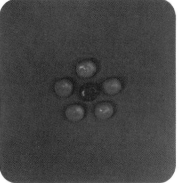

27. Enlarged picture showing piped dots for floral motif.

28. Pipe floral motif on cake-top, as shown (No. 1).

29. Pipe a dot between each cake-top shell (No.1).

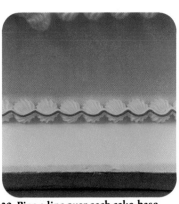

30. Pipe a line over each cake-base shell (No. 2) then overpipe each No.2 line (No.1).

31. Pipe a floral motif at the centre of each cake-side (No.1) (T).

32. Pipe curved lines around cake-board (No.2) then pipe a line beside each No.2 line (No.1) and then decorate as required.

44

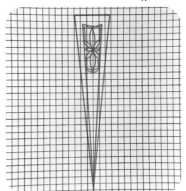

1. Drawing showing template of a section of fan.

2. Drawing showing template of the fan tassel.

3. Drawing showing part of the word 'Mother'.

4. Drawing showing the remaining part of the word 'Mother'.

5. Outline and flood-in on waxed paper the area of the fan section shown (L.D. 3 hrs) (8 required).

6. Filigree, pipe curved lines and 6-dot sequences as shown (No.1) (L.D. 2 hrs).

7. Pipe the floral motif shown (No.1) (L.D. 24 hrs).

8. Pipe tassel ropes on waxed paper, as shown (No.2).

9. Pipe further ropes, as shown (No.2).

10. Pipe remaining ropes, tassel and tassel bulb, as shown (No.2) (L.D. 12 hrs).

11. Outline each letter on waxed paper (No.1) (L.D. 1 hr).

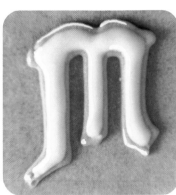

12. Flood-in letters (L.D. 24 hrs).

13. Fix a fan section to the cake top and support it at an angle until dry (L.D. 1 hr).

14. Fix and support next section, as shown (L.D. 1 hr).

15. Continue fixing and supporting sections to the left (L.D. each section 1 hr).

16. Repeat 15 to the right.

17. Pipe a ring at the fan end, as shown (L.D. 2 hrs).

18. Pipe a rope link to corner of cake, as shown (No.2).

19. Pipe curved ropes along the two top edges shown (No.42).

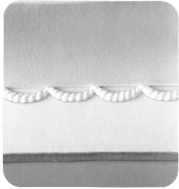

20. Pipe matching curved ropes around the whole of the cake base (No.42).

21. Pipe plain shells along the remaining two top edges (No.2).

22. Pipe graduated bulbs in each base curve (No.2).

23. Pipe a line beside the top ropes, as shown (No.2).

24. Fix letters to the cake top.

25. Pipe a floral decoration to the cake top corner shown (No.1).

26. Pipe dots against the No.2 line, as shown (No.1).

27. Pipe a floral decoration on each side of the cake (No.2) (T).

28. Pipe curved line and dots on each side of the cake, as shown (No.2) (T).

29. Pipe curved lines around the board, as shown (No.2).

30. Pipe the decorations shown against the curved board lines (No.1).

31. Fix the tassel to the cake in the position shown.

32. Fix ribbon to edge of board.

47

Rowena

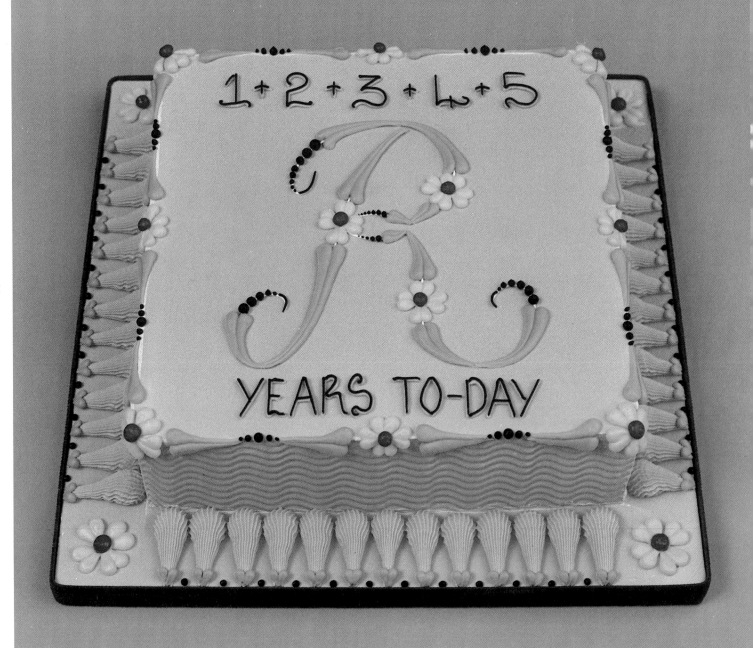

1 • 2 • 3 • 4 • 5

YEARS TO-DAY

1. Picture showing cake scraper required.

2. Use scraper when coating cake-sides to obtain pattern shown.

3. Pipe initial of choice on cake-top (No.1) in style of 'R' shown.

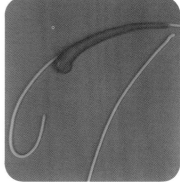

4. Pipe a long pear shape, as shown (No. 2).

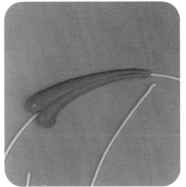

5. Pipe a further pear shape, as shown (No.2).

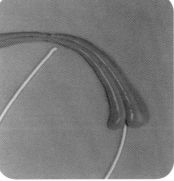

6. Pipe a pair of pear shapes, as shown (No.2).

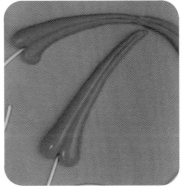

7. Pipe a further pair of pear shapes, as shown (No.2).

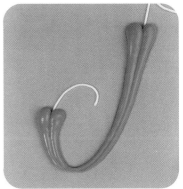

8. Pipe further pear shapes, as shown (No.2).

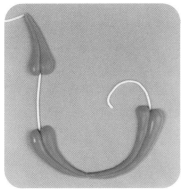

9. Pipe further pear shapes, as shown (No.2).

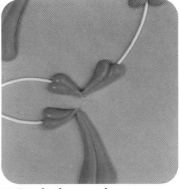

10. Pipe further pear shapes, as shown (No.2).

11. Picture showing 'R' so far.

12. Pipe floral petals, as shown (No.2).

13. Pipe further floral petals, as shown (No. 2).

14. Pipe further floral petals, as shown (No.2).

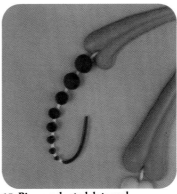

15. Pipe graduated dots and overpipe the end of the line, as shown (No.1).

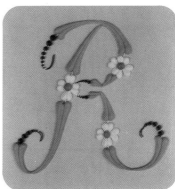

16. Repeat 15 where shown and pipe a dot to each floral centre (No.1).

49

17. Pipe message of choice on cake-top (No.2).

18. Overpipe message (No.1).

19. Pipe floral petals at each cake-top corner, as shown (No.3).

20. Pipe further floral petals at each corner, as shown (No.3).

21. Repeat 19-20 at the centre of each cake-top edge.

22. Pipe a pair of long pear shapes between each floral design (No.2).

23. Repeat 22 on cake-side, as shown.

24. Pipe a dot at each cake-top edge floral centre (No.1).

25. Pipe graduated dots between each cake-top edge pair of pear shapes (No.1).

26. Pipe a long shell on the cake-board centre (No.44).

27. Pipe long shells each side of the central shell, as shown (No.44). Repeat 26-27 on each side.

28. Pipe a pair of floral petals in position shown (No.2).

29. Repeat 28 around cake board.

30. Pipe floral petals at each cake-board corner (No.3).

31. Pipe a central dot on each cake-board floral design (No.1).

32. Pipe a dot between each pair of cake-board floral petals (No.1).

50

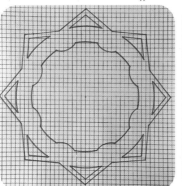

1. Drawing showing template of cake-top runout.

2. Drawing of Tracy.

3. Drawing of bird carrying parcel.

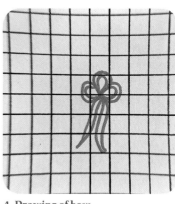

4. Drawing of bow.

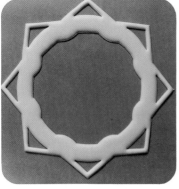

5. Outline and flood-in the runout on waxed paper (L.D. 24 hrs).

6. Pipe-in the parts of Tracy shown on waxed paper (L.D. 30 m).

7. Pipe-in the further parts of Tracy shown (L.D. 30 m).

8. Pipe-in the further parts of Tracy shown (L.D. 30 m).

9. Pipe-in the further parts of Tracy shown (L.D. 30 m).

10. Pipe-in the further parts of Tracy shown (L.D. 30 m).

11. Complete the piping of Tracy and then decorate, as shown (L.D. 24 hrs).

12. Pipe single dots along inside edge and 6-dot sequences along outer pattern edge (No.1) (L.D. 12 hrs).

13. Pipe-in bird's right wing and tail on waxed paper (No.1) (L.D. 10 m) (5 birds required).

14. Pipe-in bird's body using two colours (No.1) (L.D. 10 m).

15. Pipe-in left wing and parcel (No.1) (L.D. 24 hrs).

16. Decorate bird and parcel, as shown.

17. Pipe a flower motif in each runout triangular space (No.1) (L.D. 12 hrs).

18. Pipe a line around the top edge of the cake (No.3) (L.D. 1 hr).

19. Overpipe the No.3 line (No.2) and immediately fix runout to cake top.

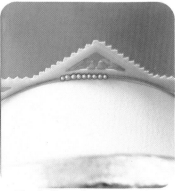

20. Pipe bulbs under runout at top edge of the cake (No.2) (T).

21. Pipe a line on the cake board to match the runout outline (No.2).

22. Flood-in between the board No.2 line and cake base (L.D. 12 hrs).

23. Pipe the bow on waxed paper (No.1) (L.D. 2 hrs) (8 required).

24. Pipe bulbs around the base of the cake (No.2).

25. Pipe a line beside the board runout (No.2).

26. Pipe a line beside the No.2 line (No.1) and then overpipe the No.2 line (No.1).

27. Fix Tracy to the cake top.

28. Fix a bird and parcel to cake top and then join parcel to beak with a piped bow (No.1).

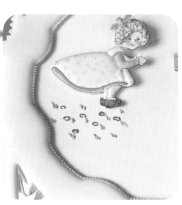

29. Pipe ground beneath Tracy's feet (No.1).

30. Pipe message of choice (No.1) and then overpipe the message (No.1).

31. Fix 4 remaining bird sets around cake side.

32. Fix bows and ribbon of choice around cake board.

Donald

1. Drawing showing template of batsman.

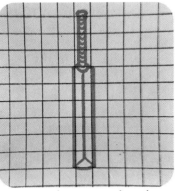

2. Drawing showing template of cricket bat.

3. Pipe-in on waxed paper the parts of the batsman shown.

4. Pipe-in the further parts shown.

5. Pipe-in the further parts shown.

6. Pipe-in the further parts shown.

7. Pipe-in the further parts shown (L.D. 2 hrs).

8. With edible colouring paint in the features shown and pipe-in the further parts shown (L.D. 24 hrs).

9. Outline and flood-in on waxed paper the part of the bat shown (L.D. 4 hrs) (32 bats required).

10. Pipe a rope to each bat to form bat handles (No.1).

11. Pipe lines on each bat, as shown (No.0) (L.D. 24 hrs).

12. Mould 4 × 1″ diameter sugar paste balls (L.D. 12 hrs).

13. Pipe two rows of 'C' lines around each ball, as shown (No.1).

14. Fix the batsman to cake-top, as shown.

15. Pipe area of grass shown (No.1).

16. Pipe message of choice to cake-top (No.2).

17. Overpipe message (No.1).

18. Pipe curved lines around message (No.1).

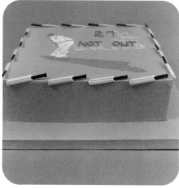

19. Fix cricket bats around cake-top edge, as shown.

20. Pipe a line around cake-base (No.44).

21. Fix cricket bats around cake-base, as shown.

22. Pipe stumps (No.3) then bails (No.2) on cake-top, as shown.

23. Pipe stumps (No.3) then bails (No.2) to each cake-side centre (T).

24. Pipe area of grass under each cake-side wicket (No.1) (T).

25. Pipe a bulb between each bat on cake-top edge (No.1).

26. Pipe a bulb between each bat on cake-base (No.1).

27. Pipe curved lines around cake-side, as shown (No.2) (T).

28. Pipe curved lines around cake-board, as shown (No.2).

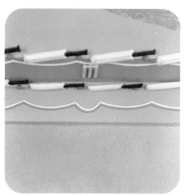

29. Pipe a line beside each cake-board No.2 line (No.1).

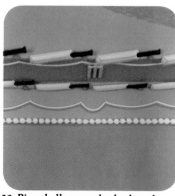

30. Pipe shells around cake-board edge (No.2).

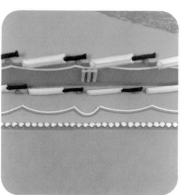

31. Pipe a line over each cake-board edge shell (No.1).

32. Fix a cricket ball to each cake-board corner.

56

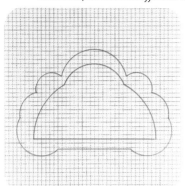

1. Drawing showing template of cake-top runout.

2. Drawing showing figure of Natalie.

3. Drawing showing template of name letters.

4. Outline cake-top runout on waxed paper, in colours shown (No.2).

5. Flood-in first colour.

6. Immediately flood-in second colour.

7. Immediately flood-in third colour (L.D. 24 hrs).

8. Pipe-in on waxed paper the parts of Natalie shown (No.1).

9. Pipe-in the further parts of Natalie shown (No.1).

10. Pipe-in or flood-in, as necessary, the parts shown.

11. Pipe-in or flood-in, as necessary, the parts shown.

12. Pipe-in or flood-in, as necessary, the parts shown (L.D. 24 hrs).

13. Pipe 24 tiny bows on waxed paper (No.0) (L.D. 24 hrs).

14. Outline and flood-in on waxed paper the name 'Natalie' (L.D. 24 hrs).

15. Complete Natalie, as shown.

16. Fix cake-top runout in exact position shown.

58

17. Fix Natalie to cake-top in position shown.

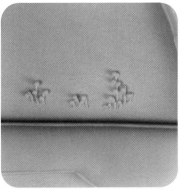

18. Pipe floral motifs along the base of the cake-top runout (No.1).

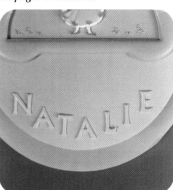

19. Position the name 'Natalie' as shown.

20. Fix the name 'Natalie' to cake-top and decorate with the piped tiny bows, as shown.

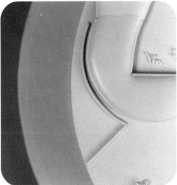

21. Pipe lines each side of the cake-top runout, as shown (No.2).

22. Pipe bulbs along front part of cake-top edge (No.2).

23. Pipe bulbs around cake-base (No.2).

24. Pipe a line over the cake-base bulbs (No.2).

25. Overpipe the cake-base No.2 line (No.1).

26. Fix ribbon around cake-side.

27. Pipe floral motif on ribbon (No.1) (T).

28. Complete floral motif on ribbon (No.1) (T).

29. Pipe curved lines around cake-board, as shown (No.2).

30. Pipe a line beside each curved cake-board line (No.1).

31. Pipe a bulb between each curved cake-board line (No.1).

32. Fix ribbon to cake-board edge and decorate, as shown.

Violet

1. Pipe a single petal to the left on waxed paper (No.57).

2. Pipe a petal to the right (No.57).

3. Pipe a petal to the lower right (No.57).

4. Pipe a petal to the lower left (No.57).

5. Pipe an overlapping petal at bottom to complete the petals (No.57).

6. Pipe in heart of violet (No.1).

7. Pipe in flower stamen (No.1). Repeat 1–7 (L.D. 24 hrs) (24 violets required).

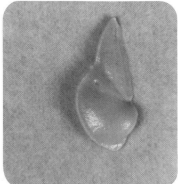

8. Pipe one side of leaf (No.57).

9. Pipe other side of leaf (No.57).

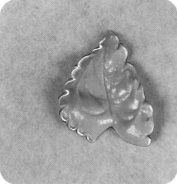

10. Etch in leaf veins with a paint brush and crimp leaf edges (12 leaves required).

11. Template.

12. Template.

13. Template.

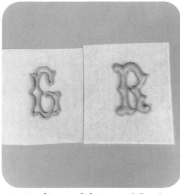

14. Outline each letter and flood-in with soft Royal Icing (No.1) (L.D. 24 hrs).

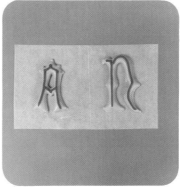

15. Overpipe each letter (No.1).

16. Place a round cake disc (of slightly smaller dimension) on cake top.

17. Using the disc as a guide, pipe a circle on cake top (No.3). Remove disc.

18. Pipe a line inside the No.3 line and then overpipe the No.3 line (No.2).

19. Pipe a line inside the No.2 line (No.1).

20. Pipe plain bulbs around top edge of cake (No.4).

21. Pipe equal sized bulbs around base of cake (No.4) (L.D. 1 hr).

22. Overpipe each top bulb with an 'S' scroll so that the tail extends onto the 2nd bulb (No.2).

23. Overpipe each base bulb with an 'S' scroll so that the tail extends onto the 2nd bulb (No.2).

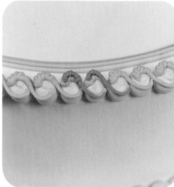

24. Overpipe all top scrolls (No.1).

25. Overpipe all base scrolls (No.1).

26. Pipe a line on cake board (No.3).

27. Pipe a line outside the No.3 line and then overpipe the No.3 line (No.2).

28. Pipe a line outside the No.2 line (No.1).

29. Pipe small scallops inside the cake top No.1 line and then outside the board No.1 line (No.1).

30. Fix letters to cake top and pipe curved flower stems (No.2).

31. Fix the violets and leaves to the stems.

32. Pipe 2 curved lines (No.2) and fix a pair of violets on cake side.

With
Very
Best
Wishes

1. Cut and place a square template on cake-top, as shown.

2. Pipe shells around template (No.42). Remove template.

3. Picture showing cake-top.

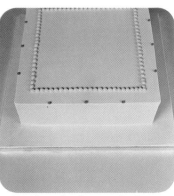

4. Divide each cake-top edge into four equal portions and mark with piped dots (No.1).

5. Pipe a scroll on cake-top corner, as shown (No.44).

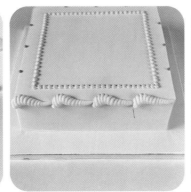

6. Continue piping scrolls along cake-top edge (No.44).

7. Repeat 5–6 along remaining edges, as shown.

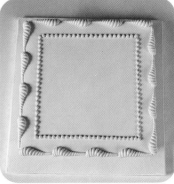

8. Picture showing cake-top.

9. Pipe shells around cake-base (No.44).

10. Picture showing size of shells at cake-base.

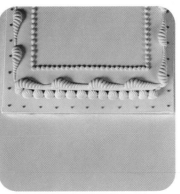

11. Divide cake-board into portions shown with piped dots (No.1).

12. Pipe a scroll between each pair of dots (No.42).

13. Picture showing completed cake-board scrolls.

14. Pipe a curved line over the first cake-top corner scroll (No.3).

15. Pipe a curved line over each of the remaining cake-top scrolls (No.3).

16. Pipe a curved line over a pair of cake-base shells (No.3).

17. Continue piping a curved line over remaining pairs of shells, as shown (No.3).

18. Picture showing stage reached so far.

19. Overpipe each cake-top No.3 curved line (No.2).

20. Overpipe each cake-base No.3 curved line (No.2).

21. Pipe the word 'With' (No.2).

22. Pipe the word 'Very' (No.2).

23. Pipe the word 'Best' (No.2).

24. Pipe the word 'Wishes' (No.2).

25. Overpipe each word (No.1).

26. Pipe curved lines on cake-top, as shown (No.1).

27. Pipe further curved lines on cake-top, as shown (No.1).

28. Pipe further curved lines on cake-top, as shown (No.1).

29. Fix flowers of choice to curved lines, as shown.

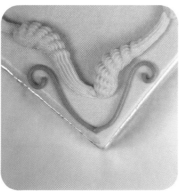

30. Pipe curved lines on each cake-board corner (No.1).

31. Fix a matching flower to each cake-board corner.

32. Pipe a dot between each cake-board scroll (No.1).

Denis

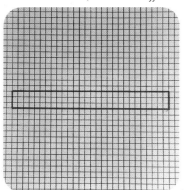

1. Drawing showing template of plaque.

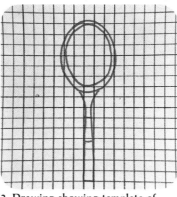

2. Drawing showing template of tennis racket.

3. Cover the area of cake-top shown, with a piece of card.

4. Spread some Royal Icing on cake-top edge.

5. Immediately stipple Royal Icing with a sponge and continue until cake-top edge is complete.

6. Remove piece of card.

7. Spread Royal Icing and stipple around cake-side and cake-board (L.D. 2 hrs).

8. Outline, and flood-in, on waxed paper, plaques (L.D. 24 hrs) (2 required).

9. Pipe racket strings, as shown, on waxed paper (No. 0) (4 required).

10. Pipe across the racket strings (No. 0).

11. Pipe a line around the strings, as shown (No. 1).

12. Flood-in between the strings and the outside line (L.D. 1 hr).

13. Outline and flood-in part of racket handle (L.D. 1 hr).

14. Outline and flood-in remaining part of racket handle (L.D. 24 hrs).

15. Paint racket as shown (with edible colouring).

16. Pipe a line on waxed paper (the width of the tennis court) (No.2).

17. Pipe vertical lines, as shown (No. 1).

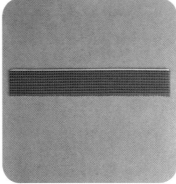

18. Pipe horizontal lines, to form net (No. 1).

19. Pipe a post to each end of net (No. 4) (L.D. 12 hrs).

20. Pipe inscription of choice to runout pieces (No. 1) and then overpipe inscription (No. 1).

21. Pipe tennis court lines, as shown (No. 2).

22. Pipe further lines, as shown (No. 2).

23. Fix inscription runouts to cake-top.

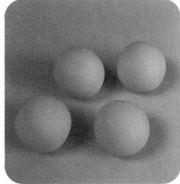

24. Mould 28 (1″ diameter) sugar paste balls.

25. Fix balls around cake-base.

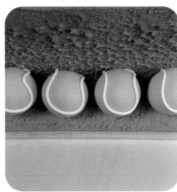

26. Pipe a line on each ball, as shown (No. 2).

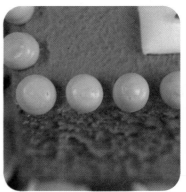

27. Pipe bulbs around cake-top edge, as shown (No. 3).

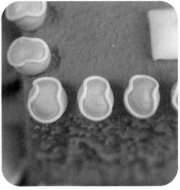

28. Pipe a line on each cake-top bulb, as shown (No. 1).

29. Picture showing cake (to compare tennis ball sizes).

30. Fix a racket to each cake-side.

31. Fix tennis net.

32. Fix figures to cake-top.

68

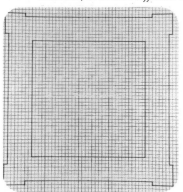

1. Drawing showing template of cake-top large runout.

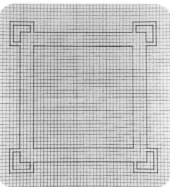

2. Drawing showing template of cake-top small runout.

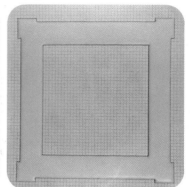

3. Outline and flood-in on waxed paper the large runout (L.D. 24 hrs).

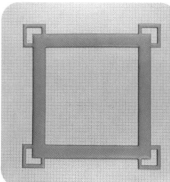

4. Outline and flood-in on waxed paper the small runout (L.D. 24 hrs).

5. Pipe shells along the inside edge of the large runout (No.0).

6. Pipe shells around outside edge of large runout (No.1).

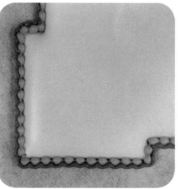

7. Pipe a line over each outside edge shell (No.0) (L.D. 24 hrs).

8. Pipe single dots along inside edge of small runout (No.1).

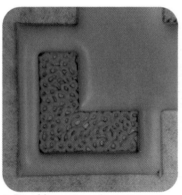

9. Pipe filigree in each small runout aperture (No.0).

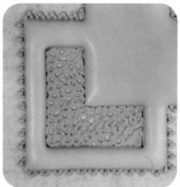

10. Pipe 3-dot sequence around outside edge of small runout (No.1) (L.D. 24 hrs).

11. Pipe lines around cake-board, as shown (No.2).

12. Flood-in between cake-base and the No.2 line (L.D. 24 hrs).

13. Pipe a line around cake-top edge (No.3) (L.D. 1 hr).

14. Carefully remove runouts from waxed paper by pulling paper over edge of table.

15. Overpipe the cake-top No.3 line (No.2).

16. Immediately fix large runout to cake-top.

17. Pipe shells between cake-top edge and runout (No.2) (T).

18. Pipe a line on top of the large runout, as shown (No.3) (L.D. 1 hr).

19. Overpipe the cake-top No.3 line (No.2).

20. Immediately fix small runout to cake-top.

21. Pipe shells around cake-base (No.3).

22. Pipe a line over each shell (No.1).

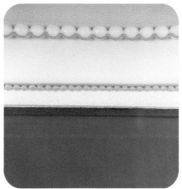

23. Pipe shells around the cake-base runout (No.1).

24. Pipe a line over each cake-base runout shell (No.0).

25. Pipe first line of inscription (No.1).

26. Pipe message (No.1).

27. Pipe shells beside first line (No.0).

28. Pipe a line over each shell (No.0).

29. Pipe the straight and curved lines shown (No.0).

30. Pipe the curved lines shown (No.1) then overpipe curved lines (No.1).

31. Decorate the curved lines (No.1).

32. Fix decorations of choice.

Yvette

NOTE: *Before attempting to decorate this cake, please study the whole sequence of photographs and notes and ensure you have the proper equipment and materials, as well as sufficient time. Additional information can be found on pages 4-14 and 96.*

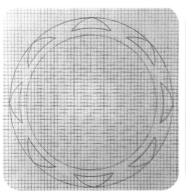

1. Drawing showing template of cake-top runout.

2. Make 14 various sized rosebuds and roses from sugar paste.

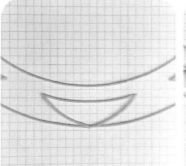

3. Outline on waxed paper the cake-top runout (No.2).

4. Flood-in the cake-top runout (L.D. 24 hrs).

5. Pipe a long leaf on waxed paper, as shown (leaf bag) and immediately place in curved position.

6. Pipe further leaf, as shown (Leaf bag) (L.D. 24 hrs).

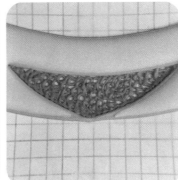

7. Pipe filigree in apertures of cake-top runout (No.0) (L.D. 24 hrs).

8. Fix cake-top runout to cake-top.

9. Pipe bulbs around cake-top edge, as shown (No.2) (T).

10. Pipe a line around cake-board (No.2).

11. Flood-in area between cake-base and No.2 line (L.D. 24 hrs).

12. Pipe curved line on cake-top, as shown (No.3).

13. Pipe further curved lines, as shown (No.2).

14. Fix piped leaves to design.

15. Pipe leaves to base of design, as shown (Leaf bag).

16. Fix two rosebuds in position shown.

17. Pipe name of choice to cake-top (No.2).

18. Overpipe name of choice (No.1).

19. Overpipe name of choice (No.0).

20. Pipe lines and curved lines in position shown (No.2).

21. Overpipe No.2 lines (No.1).

22. Pipe shells around cake-base (No.2).

23. Pipe shells around cake-board runout (No.1).

24. Pipe a line over each cake-base shell (No.1).

25. Pipe a line over each cake-board shell (No.1).

26. Overpipe each cake-base No.1 line (No.1).

27. Overpipe each cake-board No.1 line (No.1).

28. Pipe scalloped line around cake-board edge (No.1).

29. Pipe a dot in each scallop (No.1).

30. Fix various roses and buds at each cake-base quarter to form sprays.

31. Pipe curved lines at each spray (No.2) and then overpipe No.2 curved lines (No.1).

32. Pipe leaves on each spray curved line (Leaf bag).

74

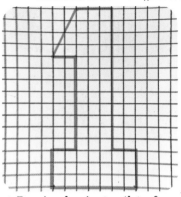

1. Drawing showing template of a figure '1'.

2. Drawing showing template of Teddy.

3. Outline and flood-in on waxed paper the figure '1' (L.D. 24 hrs).

4. Pipe a line around the top edge of the figure '1' (No.1).

5. Pipe the further lines and graduated dots shown (No.1) (L.D. 1 hr).

6. Cover the Teddy template with waxed paper and pipe-in the parts shown (L.D. 30 m).

7. Pipe-in the further parts shown (L.D. 30 m).

8. Pipe-in the further parts shown (L.D. 30 m).

9. Pipe-in the further parts shown (L.D. 24 hrs).

10. Pipe bow on waxed paper in the sequence shown (L.D. 24 hrs).

11. Pipe-in face (No.1) and paint other parts, as shown, with edible colouring.

12. Fix bow to Teddy's neck.

13. Pipe shells along one top edge of the cake (No.7).

14. Pipe 'C' lines along the adjoining edge (No.7).

15. Pipe shells along the remaining two edges (No.7).

16. Repeat 13–15 at cake base.

17. Pipe shells down each corner (No.7) (T).

18. Pipe a line beside the top shells (No.3).

19. Pipe a curved line beside the top 'C' line (No.3).

20. Overpipe the top 'C' line (No.3).

21. Overpipe the base 'C' line (No.3).

22. Overpipe the top 'C' line (No.2).

23. Pipe a dot between each top shell (No.2).

24. Repeat 22–23 on the base.

25. Fix figure '1' and Teddy to cake top.

26. Pipe message of choice (No.2).

27. Pipe curves, as shown (No.1).

28. Pictures 28–31 show sequence of piping a Teddy on each side of the cake. Pipe ears (No.3).

29. Pipe face (No.3).

30. Pipe body (No.3).

31. Pipe arms and legs (No.3) (L.D. 2 hrs).

32. Paint Teddy's features with edible colouring and fix ribbon to board edge.

Geraldine

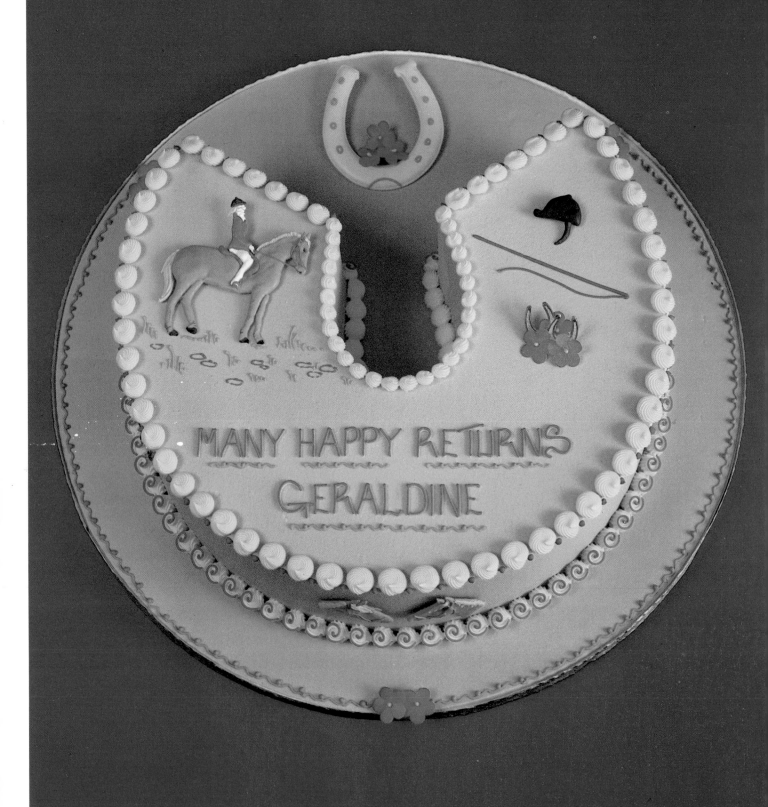

1. Drawing showing template of horse's head.

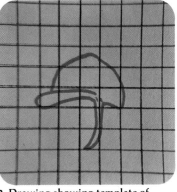

2. Drawing showing template of riding hat.

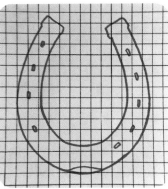

3. Drawing showing template of horseshoe.

4. Drawing showing template of horse and rider.

5. Pipe-in the parts of the horse's head shown on waxed paper (No.2).

6. Pipe-in remaining part of head (No.2) (L.D. 4 hrs).

7. Decorate horse's head, as shown (L.D. 24 hrs) (2 facing left and 2 facing right required).

8. Pipe riding hat on waxed paper (No.2) (L.D. 24 hrs).

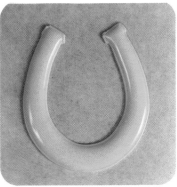

9. Outline the horseshoe on waxed paper (No.2) then flood-in (L.D. 24 hrs).

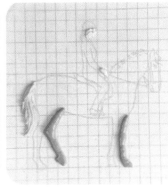

10. Pipe-in on waxed paper the parts of the horse and rider shown.

11. Pipe-in the further parts shown.

12. Pipe-in the further parts shown.

13. Pipe-in the further parts shown.

14. Pipe-in the further parts shown.

15. Decorate horeshoe, as shown (No.1).

16. Picture showing horseshoe shaped coated cake on cake-board.

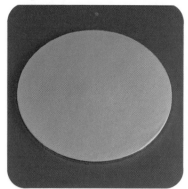

17. Coat a seperate cake-board with Royal Icing (L.D. 24 hrs).

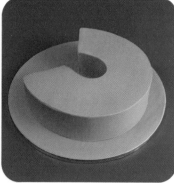

18. Transfer coated cake to coated board.

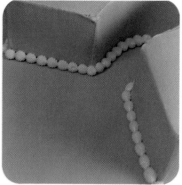

19. Pipe shells around cake-base (No.44).

20. Pipe rosettes around inside cake-top edge (No.42).

21. Pipe rosettes around outside cake-top edge (No.43).

22. Pipe a dot between each cake-top edge rosette (No.2).

23. Pipe a 'C' line on each cake-base shell (No.2) then overpipe each 'C' line (No.2).

24. Pipe whip (No.2) and fix riding hat to cake-top.

25. Fix horse and rider runout to cake-top and decorate as shown (No.1).

26. Pipe inscription of choice to cake-top (No.1) and then over-pipe inscription (No.1).

27. Pipe curved lines under inscription (No.1) and fix artificial flowers and horseshoes to cake-top, as shown.

28. Fix inward facing horse's head to each cake-end.

29. Fix remaining pair of heads to back of cake.

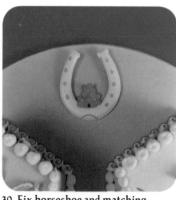

30. Fix horseshoe and matching artificial flowers to cake-board.

31. Pipe curved lines and dots around cake-board edge (No.2).

32. Fix artificial flowers and horseshoes around cake, as required.

NOTE: Before attempting to decorate this cake, please study the whole sequence of photographs and notes and ensure you have the proper equipment and materials, as well as sufficient time. Additional information can be found on pages 4-14 and 96.

1. A marzipanned and coated cake in the shape of a '5' required on a round board.

2. Roll out of a strip of sugar paste to cover the sides of the '5'.

3. Fix the sugar paste to the sides of the '5'.

4. Stipple the cake board with Royal Icing.

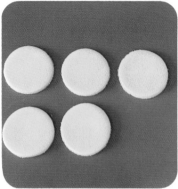

5. Roll out and cut from sugar paste 5×¾" diameter discs.

6. Moisten two discs and place on waxed paper, as shown.

7. Moisten and add a third disc, as shown.

8. Moisten and add a fourth disc, as shown.

9. Moisten and add a fifth disc, as shown.

10. Form a sugar paste dome, moisten and fix to centre of discs.

11. Shape discs to form petals (L.D. 12 hrs).

12. Repeat 5–11 in various colours to make 10 flowers.

13. Pipe a rope over the part of the dome shown (No.2).

14. Pipe eyes, as shown (No.2).

15. Pipe nose and mouth, as shown (No.2).

16. Pipe eyelids, as shown (No.2) (Repeat 13–16 on each flower). (L.D. 2 hrs).

17. Pipe rosettes around cake-top edge (No.7).

18. Pipe rosettes around cake base (No.7).

19. Pipe a curved rope beside each cake-top rosette (No.2).

20. Pipe a curved rope beside each base rosette (No.2).

21. Pipe a dot at the centre of each rosette (No.2).

22. Pipe part of the message of choice on cake top, as shown (No.2).

23. Pipe another part of the message of choice, as shown (No.2).

24. Complete message of choice, as shown (No.2).

25. Overpipe message (No.1).

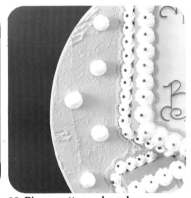

26. Pipe rosettes on board, as shown (No.7).

27. Pipe rosettes on board, as shown (No.7).

28. Fix a flower to each board rosette.

29. Repeat 28 on other side of the '5'.

30. Pipe curved lines on board (No.3); pipe a rosette centrally (No.7) and finish with a piped dot (No.2).

31. Pipe 5 shaped rings on cake top, as shown (No.2).

32. Fix a candle holder and candle in each ring and ribbon to the board edge.

Albert

NOTE: Before attempting to decorate this cake, please study the whole sequence of photographs and notes and ensure you have the proper equipment and materials, as well as sufficient time. Additional information can be found on pages 4-14 and 96.

1. A round cake and board coated in the normal way required.

2. A second board of the same size required.

3. Cover the second board with waxed paper.

4. Divide perimeter of waxed paper into 16 equal portions with piped dots (No.2).

5. Pipe a curved line between each pair of dots, as shown (No.2).

6. Upturn cake onto waxed paper and flood-in as shown (L.D. 24 hrs).

7. Upturn the cake and remove the waxed paper.

8. Pipe matching curved lines on the cake board (No.2).

9. Flood-in base of cake to the No.2 line (L.D. 12 hrs).

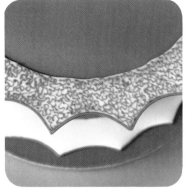

10. Filigree the top runout (No.1).

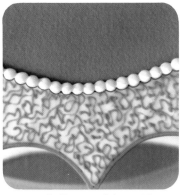

11. Pipe shells around the inside edge of the top runout (No.2).

12. Pipe shells around base of cake (No.3).

13. Overpipe the top edge shells with a line (No.1).

14. Pipe parallel lines on cake top, as shown (No.2).

15. Pipe a curved line on cake top, as shown (No.2).

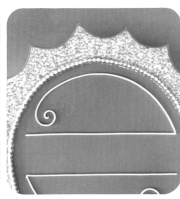

16. Pipe a second curved line, as shown (No.2).

17. Pipe a line beside each No.2 line (No.1).

18. Pipe scallops beside each No.1 line (No.1).

19. Pipe curved lines around the middle of the cake, as shown (No.2) (T).

20. Pipe a line under the cake-side No.2 line (No.1) and then pipe a line against the No.2 line (No.1) (T).

21. Pipe the vertical lines shown (No.1) (T).

22. Overpipe the base shells with a line (No.2).

23. Pipe a line beside the base runout (No.2).

24. Overpipe the base shell No.2 line (No.1).

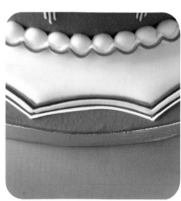

25. Pipe a line beside the board No.2 line (No.1) and then overpipe the board No.2 line (No.1).

26. Pipe a 6-dot motif at each board runout point (No.1).

27. Pipe a 6-dot motif above each cake-side line curve (No.1).

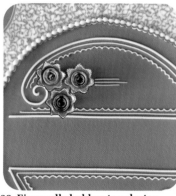

28. Fix candle holders to cake top and pipe the lines shown (No.1).

29. Pipe message of choice (No.1).

30. Pipe the 6-dot motifs shown (No.1).

31. Fix artificial flowers and pipe the lines shown (No.1).

32. Fix candles to holders and ribbon to the board edge.

1. Drawing showing template of duck.

2. Drawing showing template of rabbit.

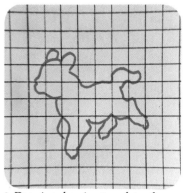

3. Drawing showing template of lamb.

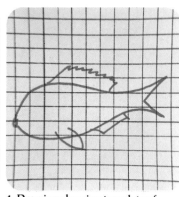

4. Drawing showing template of fish.

5. Drawing showing template of elephant.

6. Drawing showing template of dog.

7. Outline each figure on waxed paper (No.2).

8. Flood-in each figure (L.D. 24 hrs) (3 of each required).

9. Decorate duck, as shown (No.2 and No.1).

10. Decorate rabbit, as shown (No.2 and No.1).

11. Decorate lamb, as shown (No.2 and No.1).

12. Decorate fish, as shown (No.2 and No.1).

13. Decorate elephant, as shown (No.2 and No.1).

14. Decorate dog, as shown (No.2 and No.1).

15. Place cake on board and coat with one layer of Royal Icing (L.D. 24 hrs).

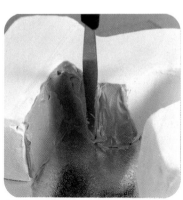

16. Spread Royal Icing around the inside of the figure '3' cake using a thin palette knife.

17. Using the thin palette knife smooth the Royal Icing with a continuous movement.

18. Remove surplus Royal Icing from cake-top and board (L.D. 2 hrs).

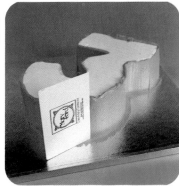

19. Coat outside of figure '3' with Royal Icing and smooth with plain scraper.

20. Remove surplus Royal Icing from cake-top and board (L.D. 12 hrs).

21. Coat cake-top and then remove surplus icing from cake-sides (L.D. 12 hrs) and then repeat 16-21.

22. Stipple cake-board with Royal Icing using a fine sponge.

23. Pipe shells around cake-base (No.7).

24. Fix runout figures around cake-side.

25. Pipe shells around cake-top edge (No.7).

26. Roll out, cut and fix a sugar paste plaque to cake-top, as shown.

27. Pipe inscription of choice on cake-top (No.2).

28. Pipe name(s) of choice on plaque (No.2).

29. Overpipe inscription (No.1) and then pipe curved lines, as shown (No.1).

30. Overpipe name(s) (No.1) then pipe curved lines, as shown (No.1).

31. Pipe shells around cake-board edge (No.5).

32. Fix artificial decorations and remaining runout figures.

NOTE: Before attempting to decorate this cake, please study the whole sequence of photographs and notes and ensure you have the proper equipment and materials, as well as sufficient time. Additional information can be found on pages 4-14 and 96.

1. Pipe assorted rosettes and bulbs of various colours (No. 42) (No. 2) (L.D. 24 hrs).

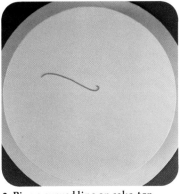

2. Pipe a curved line on cake-top, as shown (No. 1).

3. Pipe a further curved line, as shown (No. 1).

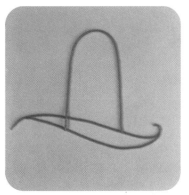

4. Pipe further curved line, as shown (No. 1).

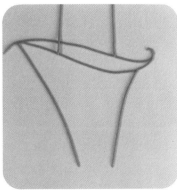

5. Pipe further curved lines, as shown (No. 1).

6. Pipe further curved lines, as shown (No. 1) to complete outline of basket.

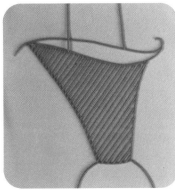

7. Pipe lines to basket side, as shown (No. 1).

8. Pipe lines at basket base (No. 1).

9. Pipe lines to back of basket, as shown (No. 1).

10. Pipe lines across the basket-side lines and back of basket lines (No. 1).

11. Pipe lines across basket-base lines (No. 1).

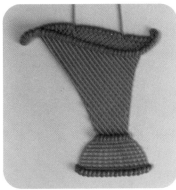

12. Pipe ropes, as shown (No. 2).

13. Pipe a rope over basket handle (No. 2) (L.D. 1 hr).

14. Fix assorted rosettes and bulbs in and over the basket, as shown.

15. Pipe leaves, as shown (Leaf bag).

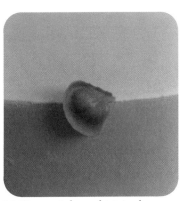

16. Pipe a petal on cake-top edge (No. 58) (equally space 16 around cake-top edge).

NOTE: *Before attempting to decorate this cake, please study the whole sequence of photographs and notes and ensure you have the proper equipment and materials, as well as sufficient time. Additional information can be found on pages 4-14 and 96.*

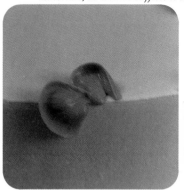

17. Pipe a second petal to each cake-top petal, as shown (No. 58).

18. Pipe a further petal, as shown (No. 58).

19. Pipe flower centre to each flower (No. 58).

20. Pipe graduated dots to each flower, as shown (No. 2).

21. Repeat 16–19 on cake-base.

22. Pipe graduated dots to each cake-board flower, as shown (No. 2).

23. Pipe curved lines around cake-side (No. 2) (T).

24. Fix assorted rosettes and bulbs to curved lines, as shown.

25. Pipe leaves to cake-side flowers (Leaf bag).

26. Pipe inscription of choice to cake-top (No. 1) and then overpipe inscription (No. 1).

27. Pipe curved lines, as shown (No. 1).

28. Pipe dots beside the curved lines shown (No. 1).

29. Pipe bow to basket handle (No. 1) and then overpipe bow (No. 1).

30. Pipe bow tails (No. 1) and then overpipe tails (No. 1).

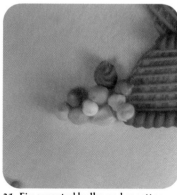

31. Fix assorted bulbs and rosettes to base of basket.

32. Pipe leaves between bulbs and rosettes (Leaf bag).

William

Many
Happy
Returns
William
With
Fondest Love
and
Every Good
Wish
For
The Future

1. An 8" square cake required.

2. Cut a section from one end.

3. Trim cut section and fix to cake, as shown.

4. Cut and trim cake to form an open book.

5. Marzipan and coat the cake on a 14" square board in the normal way.

6. Cut a template from card to match the cake top size.

7. Cut the template in half and then cut two matching sheets of waxed paper.

8. Place a bent straw on top of the cake, as shown.

9. Place one template on top of the straw and cake, as shown.

10. Coat one piece of waxed paper in Royal Icing.

11. Lay coated waxed paper on cake-top template (L.D. 24 hrs).

12. Repeat 8–11 but fix a cocktail stick to corner to form a curved page, as shown.

13. Drawing showing template of a flower.

14. Outline and flood-in on waxed paper the part of the flower shown (L.D. 30m).

15. Outline and flood-in the further parts shown (L.D. 30m).

16. Outline and flood-in the further parts shown (L.D. 30m).

NOTE: *Before attempting to decorate this cake, please study the whole sequence of photographs and notes and ensure you have the proper equipment and materials, as well as sufficient time. Additional information can be found on pages 4-14 and 96.*

17. Pipe a bulb in the centre of the flower (L.D. 24 hrs) then paint as shown in edible colouring.

18. Remove top pages and coat each side of the book using a fine comb.

19. Coat top and bottom ends of half the book using a fine comb.

20. Coat top and bottom ends of half the book using a fine comb.

21. Pipe a line on the board in the shape shown (No.2).

22. Flood-in between the line and the base of the cake (L.D. 12 hrs).

23. Pipe shells around base of cake (No.42).

24. Peel off waxed paper from pages.

25. Fix flower in the position shown and then pipe the lines, as shown (No.1).

26. Picture showing page-edge decoration.

27. Pipe the decoration as shown.

28. Pipe message of choice and decorative lines (No.1).

29. Pipe message of choice, decorative lines and page-edge decoration (No.1).

30. Fix pages to the top of the cake.

31. Pipe lines along the edge of the board runout (No.1).

32. Fix bookmark and ribbon around the edge of the board.

Index/Glossary.